Modern Work and Human Meaning

Modern Work
and
Human Meaning

by John C. Raines
and Donna C. Day-Lower

The Westminster Press
Philadelphia

Scripture quotations from the Revised Standard Version of the Bible are copyrighted 1946, 1952, © 1971, 1973 by the Division of Christian Education of the National Council of the Churches of Christ in the U.S.A. and are used by permission.

Book design by Christine Schueler

First edition

Published by The Westminster Press®
Philadelphia, Pennsylvania

PRINTED IN THE UNITED STATES OF AMERICA
2 4 6 8 9 7 5 3 1

Library of Congress Cataloging-in-Publication Data

Raines, John C.
  Modern work and human meaning.

  Bibliography: p.
  Includes index.
  1. Work. 2. Economics—Religious aspects—
Christianity. 3. Social classes—United States.
4. Distributive justice—Religious aspects—
Christianity. I. Day-Lower, Donna C., 1951–
II. Title.
BJ1498.R335 1986   241'.64   85-26370
ISBN 0-664-24703-2 (pbk.)

Contents

Preface and Acknowledgments

Most of us devote more time to our work than to any other activity. Yet we seldom stop to think about this. Ironically, it may be only when we lose our work that we first become reflective about what having a job really means to us.

That discovery took the authors of this book toward conclusions which turned out to be of fundamental importance. We started out to write a book about unemployment. We found we had to address the far broader question of work and human meaning.

Work—and how it affects the quest for human meaning and dignity—has changed dramatically in the past decades. Experts refer to this change as "the second Industrial Revolution" and to our culture as the resulting "postindustrial society." A new global economy is emerging where neighborhoods and even national borders have as little lasting meaning to investors as the constantly changing computer readouts on comparative wage rates and tax laws. Cities, regions, even whole nations are made to compete with one another as investment capital moves swiftly around the world.

Some view this change as difficult in transition but ultimately beneficial. They speak about "the information society" and "the new service economy." They see steel mills flourishing in South Korea and predict that production of computer software will soon flourish in Pittsburgh. We find such conclusions extraordinarily optimistic. In our view, the task of protecting the human meaning of work is going to require far more planned interventions than presently contemplated on Wall Street or in Washington.

We came to these conclusions gradually. Throughout our interviews with unemployed and downwardly mobile reemployed workers and their families, we heard a deeper grief than the loss or change of a job. We heard a profound sense of abandonment, of trusted but mistaken promises taking workers and their families into a situation that left them, in the end, isolated and deeply puzzled as to the meaning of what had happened to them. Our culture's public philosophy is not able to render life morally and intellectually intelligible for these new millions of Americans forced to live outside the dream. The free market and the American dream—for many the bedrock of our nation's strength—became for us, as we listened and observed, rocks covered with wet moss, slippery underfoot. Where others sought hope, we found confusion.

It is this sequence of observations, one leading to the next, that forms the outline and argument of this book. After an initial chapter presenting the overall issue and our own value perspective, we turn to an examination of unemployment and underemployment—new jobs at lower pay, with fewer benefits. Next we consider the American public philosophy and its emphasis on individual success and self-reliance. The crisis of work is a crisis of values, our culture's understanding of the nature and motivation of human behavior.

We will spend most of our time analyzing work in the United States. But because the economy is global we are compelled, finally, to address the question of justice from this wider perspective. Workers in the third world do not "take away" the jobs of workers in the first world.[1] Rather, workers everywhere face a new, very powerful, and highly mobile capital investment system that pays little attention to community or worker well-being. This is not necessarily intentional. Individual investors and managers can be well-meaning enough. But for their good intentions to become effective, the system within which they and others make their investment decisions must be changed to give greater weight—concrete leverage—to what Pope John Paul II has called "the priority of labor."[2]

In this task, the authors have been influenced by the view of our society of Reinhold Niebuhr and, more recently, the perspective on our world of the Latin American liberation theologians. As Christians and as ethicists, we find that our biblical and religious heritage lead us beyond the immediate economic crisis to an examination of the dynamics of socioeconomic class and the distribution of power. We hope this book will contribute to the growing body of literature on work and the economy coming out of the religious community and further the dialogue begun by Pope John Paul II (in his *On Human Work*) and the American and Canadian Catholic Bishops.

The two of us came to these issues by following quite separate paths. John Raines was introduced to issues of working-class Americans in 1977. There was a public transportation strike in Philadelphia, and Raines had to hitchhike to his work in the Department of Religion at Temple University. Tony Longo, a person you will hear from in considerable detail in chapter 5, stopped to give him a ride. A taped interview with Longo began an oral history project with working-class people that led eventually to a television documentary for the Public Broadcasting System on unemployment and the downwardly mobile pattern of reemployment.

Donna Day-Lower, a Presbyterian minister and more recently a seminary professor, began serving as pastor to a small congregation in a white working-class neighborhood of Boston in 1977. Written off by many as "full of Archie Bunkers," the neighborhood, she found, was made up of people fighting for dignity in the face of an economy that was rapidly eroding the precarious hold they had managed to take of the American dream. In 1981 she moved to Philadelphia and worked in the Presbytery with many more churches like those in East Boston. It was here that the authors discovered their shared interests.

At the time, our nation was in the middle of the worst recession since the Great Depression. In the entire country, the steel town of Johnstown, Pennsylvania, had the highest unemployment rate—more than 25 percent. We went to Johnstown to learn from the workers what the crisis meant. We discovered that the experience of the unemployed posed questions that echo deeply the nightmares always hovering close by the American dream: success haunted by failure; the pursuit of independence haunted by loneliness and, when things don't work out, by self-blame. We started out to learn about unemployment and in the process learned a lot about our country, its values and contradictions.

We are indebted to the people of working-class neighborhoods in Philadelphia and in Johnstown and the coal-mining communities that surround it. They shared much of themselves with us. What we have selected to present out of hundreds of hours of oral history we do not defend in terms of rigorous sampling technique. Yet we think there is accuracy in what our informants say about our society. A few of them are quoted extensively because they express with particular vividness the themes and concerns we heard from many others. Their words remain unaltered and are used with permission.

Writing in partnership proved to be an unanticipated lesson in humility. We reviewed each other's words and ideas and were not shy about wielding our red pencils. The result is a book that is better than either of us could have written alone. In the final analysis John Raines had primary responsibility for chapters 1, 3, 5, 6, and 8 and Donna Day-Lower for chapters 2, 4, and 7. The final chapter was written jointly.

Portions of this manuscript have appeared previously in *The Christian Century, Christianity and Crisis,* and *The Other Side.* Part of the oral history material is taken from a radio series entitled "A Hard Time for Dreaming" produced by WHYY-Radio (Philadelphia) in 1982 and from a television documentary aired in 1983 entitled "When a Factory Closes" produced by WITF-TV (Harrisburg) in association with the Center for Ethics and Social Policy (Philadelphia). John Raines was the project director for both efforts. Funding for the documentary came in part from the United Presbyterian Church U.S.A., the United Methodist Church, the American Baptist Churches in the U.S.A., the Pennsylvania Humanities Council, and the Philadelphia Foundation. Temple University gave John Raines a study leave in 1981, making it possible to intensify the gathering of oral history materials.

Union Seminary in New York City awarded Donna Day-Lower a Masland Fellowship in 1981–82. Research done at that time for her Master of Sacred Theology thesis ("The White Working Class and Mainline Protestantism") contributed to the development of this manuscript. Melrose-Carmel Presbyterian Church (Melrose Park, Pennsylvania) was consistently supportive of their pastor during research that often required her to travel away from the parish.

Portions of this manuscript were read by and benefited from the critical comments of William Sullivan, Rick Geruson, Larry Rasmussen, Barbara Hogan, and Barbara Wheeler. Robin Rabinowitz, Director of the Women's Alliance for Job Equity of Philadelphia, was an ongoing resource throughout the project. We are indebted to Linda Gilroy of Johnstown, Pennsylvania, who patiently deciphered hours of taped interviews and typed the transcripts; also to David Kay of Johnstown, who helped set up interviews in that city. A research grant from Temple University paid for transcription of the taped interviews.

Modern Work and Human Meaning

1

Conscience and Economics

"It affected men terrible. Just all their dreams were in that factory, going to work, supporting their family. It was taken away from them. They felt lost; they were scared; they didn't know what to do."

Phyllis Barrett is talking about her husband, Tom, who worked for twenty-three years at Eaton Corporation's forklift truck plant in Philadelphia. The Eaton Corporation continues to make forklift trucks, but in Mexico and Japan. After being out of work for two years, Tom Barrett found a new job, but at a third less pay and with far fewer benefits.

I was working in the plant, and I was complaining about the closing of the plant, and a man named Charlie Miller said to me, "Tom, don't you realize we're the last of the buffalo?" And I said, "What the hell do you mean, Charlie, we're the last of the buffalo?" And he said, "Our type of work is leaving the country and we're just like the buffalo—we're the last remaining few people who do this work with our hands and minds, and we're not going to *be* no more. Maybe in twenty or thirty years our children's children will have prosperity again, but we're the last of the workers."[1]

The Barretts illustrate a new kind of unemployment, unrelated to normal business cycles: disappearing industrial jobs. Some of those jobs, like Tom Barrett's, will go abroad. Others will simply cease to exist. As Otis Port, an editor for *Business Week* magazine, explains, "We are now on the threshold of a massive transition to robotics. There are industries that are talking about displacing tens of thousands of workers over the next twenty years by robots. I would be surprised if anywhere near half of the people who are now unemployed get their jobs back. American business has learned—is learning rapidly—how to increase productivity and do more with less." All this is inevitable, Port concludes, because *"that's the only way we're going to survive against products that are built in low-wage-rate countries."*

What does it mean, this new survival? Who survives? In the latter part of the twentieth century, a new and powerful form of political economy is emerging that is fundamentally altering the relationships between management, labor, and the local community. A *global* economy is emerging. The revolution in electronic information processing and rapid international transport has made capital highly mobile and the division of labor international. This means that first- and third-world factories compete with one another for available investment, while all around the globe the search for profits means the replacement of workers by machines.

Phyllis Barrett sees what's happening. She sees what it means for people like herself.

I lost my security. If anything major happens now, I don't know what I'm going to do. It's just sad that all these jobs are going overseas. One reason I know they're moving overseas is because they're paying the men less money. There's no union. They don't have to give them the benefits they give workers over here. So the big companies are making more money. They don't have to worry about us little people. And they don't.

It's not that simple, according to Daniel Brubeck, Director of Communications for the Eaton Corporation, which employs 50,000 people in 165 plants on six continents. "The choice," he says, "is not between manufacturing forklifts in Japan or Philadelphia. It is between manufacturing in Japan or not manufacturing at all. They have a better cost structure. It's not solely because of lower labor costs, although that is a factor. They just can beat the pants off us in making the mass-produced smaller forklift."

Has America priced itself out of international competition? Must workers in our country get used to lower pay? Many think so. Yet those who take this position seldom pause to consider the implications. Taking the paychecks of America's best-paid industrial workers out of the economy will reduce overall consumer demand. Millions of families will want to buy—but will not be able to afford—a house of their own, or computers for their kids, or the services of a private physician, or braces for their children's teeth, or a college education.

This is already happening. New jobs being created in our society are mostly at the lower end of the service economy. The areas of work predicted to produce the most jobs through the end of the century are, in the order of their rank:

Building custodians
Cashiers
Secretaries
Office clerks
Salesclerks.[2]

The Roman Catholic Bishops of Canada have spoken about this. "In effect," they say, "capital has become transnational and technology has become increasingly capital-intensive. The consequences are likely to be permanent or structural unemployment and increasing marginalization for large segments of the population in Canada and other countries." The bishops speak of this as a "deepening moral crisis," because "through these structural changes, 'capital' is reasserted as the dominant organizing principal of economic life."[3]

Many disagree with the bishops' moral reservations. The concentration of power in the hands of capital, they believe, is not only necessary, given worldwide competitive pressures, but in fact morally benign. Widespread poverty positively requires first-world investment in third-world societies, for moral reasons as well as for reasons of economic efficiency. Steel mills in Brazil, they argue, will supply wages, support families, and build communities there; Pittsburgh will become a center of international finance, where the children of former steelworkers, having become computer literate, can in their turn benefit from the new global division of labor.

How are we to assess this debate? On what religious and ethical grounds are we to establish our response to what all sides acknowledge is a profound transformation of the global economy?

As economics becomes transnational, ethics must seek an equally comprehensive basis for its analysis. What is good for the developed world cannot be at the expense of lesser developed nations, anymore than what is good for international capital can be at the expense of local community. We must begin, therefore, with a general theory of human work. What needs does work satisfy? What human excellences does work express? Only by beginning with such general questions can we establish a basis comprehensive enough to evaluate the way work gets done, not just in this country or that but in the global economy. What does it mean, we must ask, that humans work?

Only Humans Work

As a species, *Homo sapiens,* on the planet earth, we are a part of nature. Nature's rhythms—of light and darkness, of sleep and wakefulness, of heat and cold—are built into our human mythologies as surely as they are built into our biology and physiology. Still, we are a very peculiar part of nature. Only humans make the social and natural order of which we are a part an object of our reflection and planned activity. Work, in this sense, is uniquely human.

The tool symbolizes this. Tools display our distance from the world. But they also display our directedness toward the world in order to change it. We use tools constantly to transform our natural environment, suiting it to our human purposes. The tool shows our creativity and imagination—our capacity to conceive of something different from what is already established.

But tools mark not simply our increasing capacity to dominate and control nature. Tools also mark the concrete history of our "listening" to nature *through* our tools and discovering, thereby, possibilities in nature that lay hidden to us until we developed our tools sufficiently to find out what was there all along, though veiled to us. Thus what began as a primitive magnifying glass became over time first eyeglasses and then, much later, a telescope. As a result our picture of reality vastly expanded. Human learning is not simply a history of ideas but a history of human tool development that allows us to examine nature in ever more precise and effective ways. The tool, therefore, represents the unique way in which our species collaborates itself with nature—in order to learn and, from this learning, also to transform nature after the pattern of human intentions and purposes. Human work is skilled work, and becomes ever more skilled, because it uses tools.

Human work is both skilled work and shared work—work that expresses itself in ever more elaborate tools and in an ever more complex division of labor. As humans we not only make tools and use tools. Over time we evolve our making, using, and sharing of tools in more and more complex ways. The tool displays our active and collaborative, our evolving, and, therefore, our historical way of being. The most graphic example of this can be found in our early evolution as a species. The opposed thumb, the expansion of the higher brain, and our increasingly elaborate use of tools all evolved together, over millions of years. Literally, we worked our way into what we are. Working is our species' way of being and becoming.

By work we mean not only the paid work done in factories but also the unpaid work done at home; not only the work of carpenters but also the work of writers and composers. A tool can be a plow, directly expressing our purposeful activity in cultivating the natural environment. Or a tool can be a typewriter, opening up new per-

spectives of imagination, new ways of seeing ourselves, and so trans-
forming our social environment.

The opening pages of the Bible tell us that we are made in the
image of God and that our mandate is, "Be fruitful and multiply,
and fill the earth and subdue it" (Gen. 1:28). This idea of having
"dominion" gives ecology-minded persons much difficulty, sound-
ing too aggressive, too imperialistic to accurately correspond to the
elaborate interconnectedness of the biosphere. That humans have
"dominion," however, may have a more subtle meaning—namely,
that our species' way of taking up residence upon the earth is by way
of work.

Work, then, is not first of all an instrument to gain something else
—wealth, for example. Rather, work is the direct expression of a
unique human excellence, a direct expression of the way we humans
establish ourselves in this world, develop ourselves, and in a sense
perfect ourselves as a species.

We may take as an example the emergence of the ancient cities
made possible by irrigation along the riverways of the Near East.
With this evolution in technology—in tools—a new form of dwelling
together was made possible. Because irrigation made a given por-
tion of land many times more fruitful, a much more dense population was made possible. This in turn meant the end of the nomadic
life of clan and tribe. One could no longer simply walk away from
potential invaders; an irrigation system had to be defended.

Transformed tools transformed the everyday way humans lived
together. This in turn transformed human self-understanding. With
the emergence of the irrigation city, one begins to move beyond the
world of magic. As humans by the use of their tools experience their
everyday life as more predictable, more uniform and in-control,
there emerges the notion of a transcendent deity who brings rain
not just to those who correctly manipulate the magical formula but
whose mysterious intention is thought to be expressed in all rain—
which, as the Bible says, falls "on the just and on the unjust" (Matt.
5:45). As humans by their use of tools transcend their dependence
upon an unpredictable natural environment, their gods become
more transcendent. They become gods not of a single plot of land,
or of one clan, but of a stable and uniform world.[4]

In work and through work we humans express our human essence. And over time we transform and evolve that essence—biologically, technologically, and also religiously. We begin to see,
therefore, just what it means to speak of work. Work is not first of
all what we do to "make" a living. Work *is* human living—human

being and human becoming. We are uniquely a species that lives by way of skill. It is by human skill that we establish our presence upon the earth and transform and perfect that presence.

To state the positive, however, is immediately to be driven toward the negative. In their work, many people are actually alienated from their human essence. Alienated work is an intense problem. What makes it intense is that such "bad" work attacks what is centrally human in us. Bad work deprives us of a sense of personal investment in the product of our labor. In bad work we do not know ourselves as living in and through our work, we live only while we are away from work; while we are at work we seek only to endure.

In alienated work there is a systematic domination of one social class by another. Reversing the prophet Isaiah's vision of the good society (Isa. 65:21)—"they shall build houses and inhabit them; they shall plant vineyards and eat their fruit"—in alienated work, those who dwell have not built and those who eat have not planted. The work of one class becomes to appropriate to itself the fruits of labor of all others.[5]

Bad work inflates some people with pride and officiousness while others become humiliated and belittled. Rather than joining us together, work that is bad makes each the potential antagonist of the other in a situation where, it is thought, only one can win. Bad work is literally dehumanizing; we lose touch with what is distinctly human in us that we share with every other human. Instead, we become strangers living in different worlds, or enemies competing for the same world.

Alienated work is a problem—a challenge to transcend and transform—precisely because it is *not* the inevitable destiny of work. There is nothing, for example, inherently antihuman in technology, the result of toolmaking. If technology becomes alienating, it is because of who owns and controls technology. Alienated work is not some mysterious destiny. It is human work distorted by human work, and therefore within our capacity to challenge and to change.

Work as such, work as created and intended to be, joins us to the community of fellow workers. Even in alienated work, something of this remains. Even in alienated work we experience our skill as joint skill and grieve if it is taken away. Lee Thomas, whose husband, Jack, worked at the Eaton plant with Tom Barrett, describes his loss.

I think the company doesn't realize that people are not working together just to earn money. I think most people that have a job, it's like a second family for them. Most working people have two families—the family that they live with and the family that they spend their days with, that they work around. A man has lost the family that he's used to being with. He feels that he has done something wrong, that he's being punished.

Even under conditions of alienation, through work we become part of a community. And when it is taken away we grieve.

Work remains, however obscurely, a unique human dignity and the expression of a unique human connectedness—a gift each human gives to every other human and each generation gives to the next. Precisely by our working we should be drawn out of our narrow self-preoccupation and excessive self-regard into that clarity of self-perception which sees our common human journey, nourished by the creativity and sacrifice of those who labored here before us. We should be reminded that we too are part of this journey —that our time is a part of all time, and that as inheritors we are also responsible to preserve and add to this legacy, which is built up and made fruitful in human labor.

However distorted by exploitation, however alienated and alienating is work's past and present organization, this created essence of the human—this human self-development through work—remains. It is the measure of our failure. And it is the foundation of our hope.

But such an understanding of work moves in direct contradiction to the fundamental logic now guiding our society's economic decisions.

Is Greed Enough?

Teresa O'Connor is thirty-seven years old. She worked her way up from a key-punch operator making $40 a week to a position, twenty years later, as director of computer installations for a major metropolitan hospital. Her father was an invalid, and she went to work right out of high school to help support the family. Years of night school led to a college degree and, eventually, to a $32,000-a-year career—a textbook story of the American dream come true. Only that's not the story Teresa tells. She's quitting her job. She explains:

Citibank advertises in places like *Fortune* magazine and the *Wall Street Journal* that they were able to cut forty percent of their clerical force by installing data processing. Cutting forty percent of their clerical force means women are out of work! Who are the movers of paper? They're women. It's like we're the garbage collectors of all this data that we have to pass on up.

And with that function bein' automated—yep! you need less women.

I've installed new computers in two different hospitals and one manufacturing company. And invariably it is: "How many jobs can I cut?" "How many people can we lay off?"

I just cannot do it anymore. I am making an enormous amount of money. I have a very respectable job. I'm thought of as a professional. But I cannot stand it—it's too big a conflict—I am leaving that management job. I'm on the wrong side.

Teresa's decision will strike many readers as odd, because for a long time we have been willing to tell ourselves that we live in two different worlds. One is the private world of family and community, where people share common interests and standards of decency. The other is the public world of economics and politics, where power and greed hold sway. We've been willing to divide our moral lives this way because we thought it was the only realistic thing to do. And we hoped that rapid economic growth would not so much solve the moral problems of society as make them irrelevant.

The idea that economic growth can take the place of moral responsibility goes back a long way. In fact, it is the foundation of the concept of the free market. Adam Smith wrote his famous *Wealth of Nations* in order, as he said at the time (1776), to provide "hope for the poor of London." Relying upon charity might be fine to help family and friends, but a stronger medicine was needed to combat mass poverty. For that Smith looked, of all places, to the free operation of individual self-interest. The free market would transform private vice into public good. It would take greed and turn it into economic productivity. True, some might get more of this new affluence and others a good deal less. Still, all would have more than they had in the beginning. By following only the logic of profits, those controlling capital—however unintentionally—would help at last even the poor of London.

In some of the most influential lines in all of economics, Smith argued:

> Every individual is continually exerting himself to find the most advantageous employment for whatever capital he can command. It is his own advantage, indeed, and not that of society which he has in view. But the study of his own advantage naturally, or rather, necessarily leads him to prefer that employment which is most advantageous to the society. . . . In this case, as in many other cases, he is led by an invisible hand to promote an end which was no part of his intention.[6]

How was such a marvelous reversal of intentions supposed to take place? It really was quite simple, Smith thought. The one thing you can depend on is that people will be rational, even calculating, when it comes to their own self-interest. So let these self-interested consumers be associated by the free market with competing producers. Soon you will have products of high quality at the lowest possible price. Self-interest among consumers, combined with competition among producers, will transform individual greed into the fuel of an efficient economy. Owners, workers, everyone wins—automatically, for Smith—without conscious moral intent.

For the life hereafter one may need charity and self-discipline. But for the good life here and now, such virtues can be done without—indeed, can be better done without. Smith argued that the free market permits a beneficial moral modesty, which trusts people acting in pursuit of their own self-interest far more than it trusts avowals of disinterested benevolence or claims to morally superior rights. Beyond relationships of intimacy, humans cannot be trusted with interests other than their own. Happily, however, the free market means we do not have to trust them—or prove ourselves trustworthy. For Smith, or for that part of Smith's thought most remembered and influential, the Teresa O'Connors of the world need not unite because there is no need for a battle.[7]

Thus, from the beginning of free-market thought, a wedge was driven between ethics and economics. Conscience is preserved in the private world, but in the public world of finance it is replaced by the automatic, morally unintended, but supposedly unyieldingly beneficent results of free-market competition. Just how firmly this wedge was driven is shown by the fact that the British economist Lord Keynes, who otherwise had many differences with his distant predecessor, nevertheless on this key point remained in perfect accord. In 1930, in the middle of the Great Depression, he speculated about a time, perhaps for his grandchildren, when everybody would be rich. "But beware!" Keynes warned:

> The time for all this is not yet. For at least another hundred years we must pretend to ourselves and to everyone that fair is foul and foul is fair; for foul is useful and fair is not. Avarice and usury and precaution must be our gods for a little longer still. For only they can lead us out of the tunnel of economic necessity into daylight.[8]

Keynes shared not at all Smith's passion for an unregulated market. But he did share his predecessor's trust that private greed can produce public good, a trust which sets economics at a remote distance from ethics.

Now the devastating truth is that behind this so-called realism is quite another reality. It is the reality that once human greed is set loose without conscious moral limit, it will use its power to gain special concessions in market competition—concessions leading to monopoly capitalism. Harvard economist John Kenneth Galbraith argues that a system of powerful multinational corporations has emerged, which can dominate the older market system and set the terms of exchange, while smaller businesses find they have less and less effective power.[9] Moreover, managers of capital may cease *making* much of anything at all, except more capital, by turning their attention from production to acquisitions, mergers, and money market manipulations. Profits improve, but the capacity to produce becomes obsolete.

All these problems are made more acute under the conditions of a global economy. Profits made in one country do not necessarily stay in that country to produce jobs there, but instead can flee to lower-wage-rate areas. This happened in Pittsburgh recently, where the same bank that manages the pension funds for the steelworkers' union made a major loan to build a technologically highly sophis- ticated steel mill in South Korea. The result? Yesterday's profits made-in-America and the delayed wages (the pensions) of American workers create jobs abroad and close steel mills and coal mines at home. American banks prosper, but American society does not.

The new global economy is forcing us to recognize a more funda- mental truth: deeper in us than selfishness is our vulnerability and need for community. A decent neighborhood, for example, is the product of people who find that they have a *common interest*, a good which is good not as they individually own it but as they share and preserve it with others. In our everyday life we know that greed does not generate public good. Quite the opposite: greed, unhindered by social constraint, encourages cynicism and undermines concern and care for others. Glenn Schreffler, a thirty-eight-year-old worker at the Eaton plant that closed in Philadelphia, talked of this:

It's not just four hundred and twenty workers they're hurting. You have people there who are community-oriented; they partici- pate in their community. Once the plant closes, they lose all faith in everything. They stop attending VFW meetings. They stop at- tending CYO meetings, where they can help the children on a track team, or a basketball team, or a football team. They figure, "Let somebody else do it!"

Such loss of jobs and morale inflicts costs upon community which capital does not even count.

Beyond these social injuries, the curtain of silence drawn between ethics and economics results in costs to individual human consciences. There are costs to the consciences of well-meaning men and women in business, who say, in all sincerity, "Business decisions have nothing to do with morality." There are costs to the consciences of managers, who view workers not as human persons— indeed, fellow workers—but as abstract figures in computer printouts, mere mathematical entities subject to cool-eyed managerial restructuring.

At the other end, there are costs to the consciences of workers, who come to see themselves as passive consumers of paychecks and workplace orders given by others, rather than as active participants in the common enterprise of productive effort. The "I-don't-live-here-I-just-work-here" attitude of some workers reveals a profound alienation from work, from pride in skill.

Finally, besides injury to conscience and to community, this separation of capital decisions from their human consequences leads eventually, as it must, to severe losses in long-range economic productivity. For good or for ill, work is a common effort and reaps a common consequence. When managers view the workplace as a location for piling up short-term bottom-line profits and then abandon the scene, there are long-term costs. According to David Joys of the Russell Reynolds Consulting Firm in New York City:

> I know—we all know—of people all over this town who are running their companies into the ground, taking huge, quick profits and leaving them a shell. And when you look at their contracts it's easy to see why. What does it matter to them what happens ten years from now? They're building giant personal fortunes, and *appear* to be running their companies terrifically, and in ten years, when there's nothing left, they'll be long gone.[10]

Acknowledged or unacknowledged, capital, workers, and community are joint partners. To deny that fact is not hard-nosed practicality. It is a crackpot "realism" that ultimately will impoverish us all.

The Protection of Shared Skills

Our initial claim was that only a general theory of human work can evaluate both work in the third world and work in the first world from the same point of view, from a common ethical perspective. If work indeed primarily concerns the generation of wealth, thereby securing the material basis for human life, Adam Smith may well be our best guide. But if, as we have argued, work is even more funda- mentally our species' way of establishing our presence upon the earth—if work expresses our unique human being and becoming— then another value besides wealth must provide the guiding logic of work's organization.

Human work is the preservation and enhancement of shared skills. This definition more accurately corresponds to the full meaning of human work and therefore provides a more adequate ethical norm by which to judge the organization of human labor. In the context of the new global economy, what does the preservation and en- hancement of shared skills mean?

First-world investment in third-world societies, organized as it presently is under the logic of private profits, often has the effect, however unintended, of "de-skilling" rural populations. The intro- duction of capital-intensive farming and the raising of crops for export means that land which once provided subsistence for peasant families becomes "too valuable" for those families to afford. They lose their land and have to work under the direction of and for the profit of another.

For the rural masses of the third world, this sharply increases their experience of dependency—of needing the skills of another and having "no skill" of their own. Only the landlord "knows": knows how to get capital to buy tractors and hybrid seed, together with the extensive fertilization it requires; how to buy trucks to transport the resulting high-volume crop to markets in distant cities, to tables in other lands. What small farmers—men and women—once knew no longer seems valuable. A suddenly and profoundly transformed everyday environment renders them "ignorant." They have noth- ing, they think, to teach their children—no gifts to give. Literally, they are demoralized. They can no longer grasp their life as a moral task and calling.[11]

Cities draw displaced rural populations with the promise of jobs and by the life-styles seen on television. But once they reach the city, most find no steady work. Or the work is offered only or mostly to women because they have been taught by their culture to expect less, to be more docile, and because they are more likely to be conveniently short-term workers who will eventually leave their jobs without pensions or benefits for marriage and child care. Early in the morning women leave for work in factories where there is no job security, no worker safety, no union. Later, the children go to work

—sometimes hustling in the streets. Men, finding no work, lose their place in the household economy and often abandon their families. Or people are forced to consider options for survival that are offensive to their culture and their conscience. They steal, deal in drugs, or enter into prostitution. All around the luxury hotels, where first and third worlds meet, this moral degradation is reenacted daily. Cities become the graveyards of what once was the functioning structure of traditional family life. However morally flawed the sex-role stereotyping was in that traditional family, what is left behind in the cities is something even more degrading.

Men, women, and children have been deprived of their shared skills, of their way of depending upon and contributing to one another. When looked at from the perspective of the enhancement of human skills, the price of capital investment in the third world that is governed solely or primarily by the logic of profits has proved excessively expensive.

Much of this analysis can be applied with equal appropriateness to first-world societies. The black and Hispanic underclasses in America are mirror images of third-world impoverishment and the de-skilling of multiple generations. Added to this must be the fact that workers in well-paying blue-collar jobs have recently become candidates for displacement, either because that work is shipped overseas to cheaper labor markets or because human workers are replaced by machines. An economic recovery that is simply a recovery of capital, a recovery of profits, can in fact speed up this process.

This structural contradiction—that labor must sell its work to capital in order to make a wage but can do so only where capital makes a profit, which in turn increases the power of capital over against labor—this contradiction was obscured as long as the production of wealth was confined within national boundaries and thus could trickle down. But the new "trickle out" of sending jobs offshore and adopting a technology that replaces humans with machines is bringing this contradiction in power relationships between capital and labor into sharper focus.

Since capital is the distinct winner in the first stage of this struggle, it means that first- and third-world societies increasingly reflect one another. Whether it be blacks and Hispanics or displaced steel or manufacturing workers, they experience the same demoralization, the same attack upon family interdependence and community well-being as peasants displaced from their farms in Latin America and the Philippines. Here is how one worker described a working-class neighborhood in Philadelphia where he grew up, a neighborhood now of empty factories.

It looks like . . . ah, hornets—like you see in the movies—have just gone and devastated that particular area, leaving behind people that are unemployed, that can't get jobs. The kids are all drinking beer. I guess it's due to the fact that the father can't provide. And they look at their father and say, "Well, who the hell are you?"—you know. "You're a bum in the park." Consequently, the kids just have no respect. The father can't hold his head with some sort of dignity and say, "Hey, I'm the breadwinner—you do whatever I say."

This demoralization affects not only the unemployed but the *under*employed—people displaced from well-paying jobs who have to go back to work for significantly less income, or their children who enter a service economy where the average weekly wage is sharply lower than factory work—jobs that have little security and few benefits. The wife of a dockworker living in South Philadelphia told us of the sadness that weighs upon a father who has to tell his son that he can't expect to follow his dad onto the docks, that because of containerization there won't be enough jobs. "For middle-class people," she said, "hope means change; but for working people hope is when things stay the same." Says economist Barry Bluestone of Boston College:

What it means for our society is that workers who have always believed in the American way of life, have always believed that if they worked hard, if they played according to the rules of the game, they would have a better way of life in the future than they have today—for those workers we're finding that the American dream is shattered.[12]

When people's dreams shatter, they shatter inside families and between generations. The system of passing on good work to the kids, of leaving them a home, mortgage paid off, whose value is maintained both because neighborhoods remain financially stable and because women work at maintaining neighborhood decency and the moral education of children—this way of displaying skill in parenting, of keeping faith between the generations, is shattering.

Millions of American workers—men and women—feel that their skills, once valuable, are no longer needed, that society has passed them by, that they have lost their skill because it is no longer valued. A sense of failure, of nostalgia for better days, replaces dreams that have stopped working. Sociologically and psychologically, the third world mirrors itself more and more in the first.

In the next three chapters we will explore the world of the unemployed and underemployed. They are excellent instructors in the human meaning of work, because it is when work becomes the central, the inescapable, the overwhelming problem of one's life—a problem that redefines all the things one used to think of as one's problems—that we are forced to experience, from its negative side, the meanings we and others attach to work. It is in loss and grief that we become most clear about what we had, took for granted, and have no longer.

Those of us who are employed, especially if we are relatively well employed, need to see what the new economic realities look like from the perspective of those who cannot escape the injury these new economic realities are causing. Without the moral accuracy such a perspective provides, there can be no effective public policy response. Not seeing, not hearing, we will not respond. Or we will think, quite erroneously, that we and they are on different journeys, moving toward separate destinies, rather than being members of the same society, bound together by a common future.

2

A Culture
of Disappointment

The train was pulling out of Johnstown, Pennsylvania, past the idle factories, past the autumn mountainside red with leaves the hue of iron ash, under the steel-gray sky now unpolluted by smoke, and along the innocuous-looking little stream that had drowned the dreams of so many who believed so much. We were leaving a world where we had gone, tape recorders in hand, to hear the individual stories of the unemployed and the underemployed. We had found much more. Economic crisis is not just an individual or family experience, it is a social reality as well. It was in the context of a community and its culture that the personal dreams we heard had been nurtured and the values behind them reinforced. The heaviness of the fall sky that day reflected not only the economic depression hanging over the families of Johnstown but the passing of a whole way of life.

Historically, there was a sense of invulnerability about Johnstown: a certainty, a predictability, a shieldedness. No city was ever more nestled in the ancient protection of the mountains. As the old Sunday school tune goes, "The wise man built his house upon the rock."

But Johnstown was struck by two devastating floods, one in the late nineteenth century and another in the 1930s. The high-water marks of these two floods still remain on the stone face of City Hall. The Army Corps of Engineers then fortified the banks of the river running through town. The challenge to the city's invulnerability presented by the floods was translated into an even stronger sense of survivorship. The Chamber of Commerce dubbed Johnstown "The Flood-Free City," a name that stuck. As with the wise man's house in the chorus,

> The rains came down and the floods came up,
> But the house upon the rock stood firm.

Besides the mountains and the flood walls, there was another fortress: Bethlehem Steel. Its massive and diverse factories were built along the river, and the town grew in between the cracks. Small mining towns proliferated, satellite communities that were intrinsically related to Bethlehem for life and development. As the company expanded and the local economy solidified, the smokestacks stood as living monuments to American ingenuity, free enterprise, limitless growth, infinite possibility. For this reason Johnstown attracted large numbers of Eastern Europeans who, having passed by the Statue of Liberty, came directly to Johnstown as their hometown in the Promised Land of industrial productivity and individual opportunity.

Bethlehem Steel came to define almost every aspect of life in Johnstown: the meaning and dignity of work, the definition of socioeconomic class, the shape of human relations, the scope of visions for the future. Steel built churches and provided medical care. Steel counseled alcoholics and wrought "justice" in the courts. Steel mortgaged homes and put turkeys on the table. All other institutions and businesses were dependent on Bethlehem Steel, if they were not outright extensions of it. The economy and the culture of the city were integrated, even with the ethnic diversity of the population. Both revolved around Bethlehem Steel Corporation and what it stood for as a promise for the future.

If life in Johnstown was not always easy, it was at least predictable. There was a lot one could count on. There would always be jobs at the mill, and incomes would increase. For every layoff, there would be a callback. There were houses to buy, power to be had through the union, a big church wedding to be planned, children to be delivered and baptized. The next generation would have a little more of all of it—perhaps even a college diploma. Calloused hands and tired backs were a small price to pay for this American dream. The daily indignities experienced by the mill hunks were absorbed in the larger headiness of participating in the industrial venture upon which the whole country—indeed, the whole industrial world —depended. Ingots of pride and hope were forged daily. The substance of life and the stuff of the dream were no less solid than steel.

The American dream picked up momentum over the years. The roots put down by the immigrants went deeper into the western Pennsylvania soil with each succeeding generation. Polish, Ukrainian, Lithuanian, Greek, and Russian Orthodox steeples testified to the social cohesion that bound families to place. Burned mortgages were trophies of hard work and dowry for the future. Looking out on a landscape bounded by the mountains and a cityscape pierced by smokestacks and church steeples, one Johnstown resident observed, "All we know and all we've ever cared about is what we can see." Johnstown seemed enough unto itself, its world solid, firmly in place. Through the growth of industry a culture had been created, a culture whose elements were hope and hard work, predictability and survivorship. In what was to prove an ironic contradiction to the thinly masked dependency on the benevolent provider, Bethlehem Steel, there was also a strong sense of self-determination and self-sufficiency.

But the house upon the rock that steel had built fell. In 1977, the rains came down yet a third time and the floods came up again—this time washing through the homes, businesses, and factories of central Johnstown as never before. Today the only graffiti in town is a spray-painted expression of disgust on the river's cement bulwarks: FLOOD-FREE MY ASS! A third high-water mark is now on City Hall. In people's minds it marks the beginning of the end. The flood exposed the foundations of Bethlehem Steel to be laid upon sand.

Before the flood of 1977 there had already been signs of erosion. In the early 1960s, Bethlehem employed a workforce of 18,000. By 1971, it was down to 16,000. As the automobile and rail markets declined, incremental cutbacks came with increasing regularity. But the flood proved to be the watershed. With depressed demand for steel at home and soaring foreign competition, Bethlehem decided not to salvage its damaged capital in Johnstown. In 1984 there were fewer than 2,000 people on the Bethlehem payroll—a veritable skeleton crew in relation to the activity of the boom years. Rumors of further layoffs continue to fly around the city and are eventually confirmed.

Bethlehem's problems have had a ripple effect on the local economy. As telephone bills are harder to pay and communication for many becomes an unaffordable luxury, telephone operators and service people join the unemployment lines. The United Way contributions thermometer no longer gushes over the top; it barely rises, forcing the paring of much-needed community services. Community health programs, such as that for victims of black lung disease, have been forced to close. Even the bars, which for a while helped dull the pain, have fallen on hard times. An "act of God" and a corporate decision are identified with the beginning of a process that will leave to rust not just the economy of Johnstown but its culture.

Gone is the predictability and the invulnerability that were woven into the old way of life. Even the sense of survivorship is on the wane. Dave Kay is the son of a steelworker who was able to go to college on a football scholarship. He returned to Johnstown to direct the black lung program. His diploma, however, did not protect him from seeing his dreams washed away.

I think the difference is that with the flood, you were short-term: you knew that you were coming back. In a matter of two or three days, the mud would be gone. The dirt would be gone. Maybe the effects would be there: the loss of a son, the loss of a family member. That would be perpetuated.

With unemployment, it's been here for two years now. Nobody has any idea. The short-term effects are gone now. I'm looking long-term, and I think that the mood has changed. [When] my dad was laid off [we'd say], "Oh, hell, don't worry, you'll get back. They'll take care of you." I think it's different now.

Faith in the dream dies hard. What may be obvious to the outsider is unspeakable in Johnstown. To the home folks, the inevitable is the unthinkable. Workers who have been laid off for as long as four or five years are just beginning to acknowledge that the callbacks they have counted on, then desperately hoped for, will not be coming. Former miners and steelworkers are just admitting to themselves, after years of discouraging job news, that the "odd jobs" they were able to find—doing a neighbor's carpentry or flipping hamburgers at McDonald's—are no longer temporary measures but define their future.

One has only to spend an afternoon in downtown Johnstown to hear and feel a community that is taking on a new understanding of itself and a new perspective on the rest of the world. Walking into a small coffee shop at lunchtime, we were greeted with a friendly inquiry now typical in Johnstown: not "Nice day, isn't it?" but "So, you folks working?" Employment is more of a shared concern than the weather, as reflected even in small talk. The staggering of the local economy has invaded everyone's experience. Cultural cues of language, symbols, and social behavior indicate a changing social context which is now marked by (1) a sense of victimization, (2) increasing isolation and class division, and (3) a fatalistic worldview.

The Community as Victim

To feel victimized is to focus on particular circumstances, on a visible villain. As does the victim of a crime or disease, one can point to a particular cause or moment when one's well-being was suddenly in the hands of a malevolent force or person. But eventually, the experience of being victimized can become personalized and generalized into a new self-perception: "I was a victim" (of another's action) becomes "I *am* a victim"—vulnerable and powerless in the world. Before it was the other who was the target of anger and resentment. Now it is the self.

Particular expressions of speech used in Johnstown betray this new self-identity as victim. Two striking examples are the constant use of the phrase "jerked around" and of the term "downgraded" when referring to one's experience. The first figure of speech calls forth the image of a fish on a line. In spite of its pulling and thrashing, the predator on the other end of the line has absolute power to manipulate its victim. When a company will not tell its employees of its future plans, when householders are referred from one agency to another in trying to secure emergency services for their family, or when union officials negotiate concessions and job reclassifications in an attempt to salvage employment for their members, one is being jerked around. In the frequent use of this sad image, the frustration of individual and collective powerlessness is communicated. In spite of the old belief in self-determination, the new perception is that of being out of control.

Being downgraded is an equally graphic expression. It is used often, usually in the context of describing situations that remind the speakers of their own downward mobility—the welfare office, the unemployment line, or standing in the grocery store line with food stamps. To be downgraded economically is equated with having one's dignity taken down a notch. Through hard work and "following the game plan," a family was supposed to be able to climb a few rungs on the socioeconomic ladder in its lifetime. To have those rungs broken has consequences for the family finances, but even more for one's sense of dignity. Mary Duranko, mother of three children and wife of a steelworker who, when we first interviewed her, had been laid off for two years, felt downgraded when she went to a religious charity for the first time:

I went down there, looked for a pair of shoes for my kid. I found a pair that would fit him and I explained to them I didn't have any money. I said, "Could I take these shoes for my son and then I'll pay for them as soon as I get my welfare check?" They wouldn't do it. They downgraded me. And I start crying. I says, "Hey I need these for my *kid.*" And they still would not gimme them shoes. So finally, my sister-in-law paid for them. They were four dollars. . . . How bad can you really go? I mean, that really woke me up, y'know, to how bad it really is when you go for charity and you can't get it. You're downgraded.

Being downgraded is the feeling which enters the gap between a belief in self-sufficiency and the reality that one cannot protect oneself. It is used in everyday conversation with absolute accuracy.

To be jerked around or downgraded is part of the warp and woof of life in Johnstown these days. People view themselves as victims, unable to defend themselves or their families and neighborhoods.

Isolation

At first glance, it would seem that the shared experience of an economic crisis would have a bonding effect, *creating* community. After all, Johnstown does have a history of working together; it shoveled itself out of the mud of three floods. There are many stories, which witness still today to a reality now rapidly fading, of neighbors helping neighbors, reminiscent of the Great Depression. Dave Kay:

I put in a new driveway in the summer. I'd been waiting to put a driveway in for years. So I mentioned it to a neighbor about six o'clock in the evening that I was going to start laying this driveway at nine o'clock in the morning. By the time I was done, I had five people there I had never even talked to: all laid-off guys from the neighborhood.

Camaraderie, yes. But I think it goes farther than that. I think it's dependence. I think it's dependence in the sense that it's all they have to look forward to. See what I mean?

Kay speaks of a lost sense of power, the ghost of a once self-confident community. Unlike the 1930s, there are social forces today that separate and isolate neighbors from each other. In the hard times of the Great Depression, industry and community suffered together. Today, industry can escape harder times and prosper elsewhere, as U.S. Steel has done by purchasing Marathon Oil. Today, when a company pulls its capital out of a community, the community is left behind to suffer, its viability threatened, and not just because of a lost economic base. The nature of interpersonal relationships, which are the glue of any community, are affected. Sometimes the patterns of human relationships are irreparably damaged. The second mark of the culture of disappointment, therefore, is the movement away from interdependency toward isolation.

Despite examples of solidarity and mutual encouragement between the families of the unemployed, walls between people are being built. Each family must necessarily concern itself with its own survival. Former co-workers are now seen as competitors for the handful of jobs that become available. In July of 1984, the year of economic recovery, 10,000 people in Johnstown applied to take the postal workers' examination—even though there were no job openings with the post office—in the hope that individual positions might become available in future through attrition. As applicants bought study guides and prepared for the exam, each was trying to outscore the next in the desperate scramble for jobs.

This competition has produced a cycle of guilt and resentment between the still-haves and the new have-nots. When Pat Gilroy still had a job at Bethlehem Steel in the security department, he ran into two of his former co-workers and described what happened:

They're very standoffish to you, very envious that you're still working and they're not. I had to take the initiative and go to them and shake their hands. Otherwise, they wouldn't have even talked to me. Other men at work, they've run into it. Actual downright animosity. Neighbors' wives have been very hostile to them because they're still working and their husbands not.

Sandy's forty-one-year-old husband had been laid off from the mill for three years. It was hard to see a younger man in the neighborhood getting called back to work while her husband was left at home:

I was really mad because . . . he's only about my age [twenty-six], so he hasn't worked in the mill that long. And he got called back to work two or three months ago. I was really upset over it. I mean, God bless them that he's going back to work, he deserves it too, but I felt really bad. 'Cause I thought my husband should have been called back before him, 'cause my husband worked longer than him. I was jealous, but I wasn't like spiteful toward her or anything. I mean I would wave or say hello . . . but still I was jealous.

The bonds of community are being strained. The old camaraderie of competition on the way up, rising on a tide that raises all boats, is lost—and it is missed.

There have always been class divisions in Johnstown. But these too seemed to intensify and isolate people even further during the new hard times. In the old culture, the culture of good times long before the Flood of '77 and the subsequent economic decline, Johnstown maintained a carefully balanced social class structure. There was a firmly entrenched caste system: "old money," bosses, middle management, and working class. Upward mobility was literally, as well as economically, a descriptive term. Those on the bottom *lived* at the bottom, in the valley, closest to the factories and furnaces. As one moved up the socioeconomic ladder, one moved notch by notch uphill to outlying areas. It was those in the valley who were hit first and hardest by the flood and then the depression. The common perception is that those at the top of the hill are also at the top of the heap and are untouched by bad times, natural or economic. This might have been true of the floods, but not of the present economic crisis.

Linda and Pat Gilroy made it up the hill on Pat's salary at the mill. Their dream house is in Westmont, a suburb laden with symbolism in Johnstown society. Pat says:

We had a talk about this at a party and it's funny, they all said, if somebody asked where they lived, they'll talk all around it—"I live in Southmont or Upper Yoder"—but they won't say Westmont 'cause they know they'll get animosity. Westmont is depicted as rich people—have everything; people in the valley have nothing. . . . When we first moved up here, there were men at work that actually quit speaking to me. . . . What really hurt me was when my brother and sister came to visit me, and even they gave me digs about movin' up here. It just blew my mind.

Linda describes what she calls the "Johnstown mentality"—the perception of social class.

It's the supervisor/millworker, we/they attitude; it's the Westmont/Johnstown, we/they attitude. A major department store in Johnstown is called Glosser Brothers, and the Glossers live here in Westmont. Therefore, everyone assumes that those who live in Westmont are "Glossers," they're all rich. When I was little and grew up in the West End, I thought "Westmont," you had to be very, very wealthy to live in Westmont.

Even in the midst of an economic crisis that has served to have a financial leveling effect on the classes, the "we/theyness" Linda describes has been preserved. There has not been a leveling of social class consciousness.

Often, for example, those dealing with their own survival expressed pity for those whom they perceived as less fortunate. But in some ways, usually unacknowledged, they needed the others to be there and *remain* less fortunate. Our own suffering is a little easier to endure if there are those who are even worse off than we are. Michael Lewis, in his book *The Culture of Inequality*, [1] describes this social dynamic. He sets the stage for his thesis by discussing the "myth of equal opportunity": that is, that everyone born in this country, regardless of socioeconomic context, has an equal opportunity to succeed through determination and hard work. Individuals set their sights and raise their aspirations, only to confront the reality of their actual achievements. The individual is then left to interpret and justify the disparity between aspirations (dreams) and achievements (reality).

Lewis contends, however, that this perception of one's own "aspiration-achievement disparity" is too painful to sustain. Therefore, individuals formulate other strategies for reinterpreting their apparent failure. Rather than blaming outside forces or lowering one's aspirations (that comes in the next generation), the most effective psychological strategy is to inflate one's achievements. This is done through a variety of means: gaining status through voluntary organizations or living through one's dreams for one's children. But by far the most prevalent strategy is to inflate one's achievements by deflating those of others. "If people are not the successes they hoped to be, they may nevertheless take comfort in the belief that they are not the failures that they might have been and that others —for want of effort and competence—*are.*"[2] In good times this means that we need to feel superior to someone, if even slightly, so that we can feel more like a success in contrast to someone else's failure. ("I may not be a foreman, but at least I'm *working*—not like those lazy welfare chiselers.") In hard times, when a whole community is feeling downgraded, economically and psychologically, it is even more important to find others you can look down on, in sympathy . . . and in superiority.

Thus the preservation of the social pecking order serves to separate neighbors from one another at a time when they need each other the most. Even in the midst of economic depression, there will always be "someone who has it a little harder than I do; they will get my sympathy and my guilt, but God I'm glad they're there. Things could be so much worse. They remind me of just how lucky I am."

Because of this dynamic, one of the ways that class consciousness and interclass tension have been acted out in Johnstown is in the arena of social service agencies. The lines drawn during the times of prosperity were brought into bold relief in a Johnstown "charity war."

After what was for Mary Duranko the humiliating experience of getting shoes for her children at the local charity, she decided to organize her own agency—an agency run by and for the families of steelworkers. The Wives' Action Committee for Unemployed Steelworkers was born out of a first meeting in March of 1982. At that meeting, which was held during the peak of unemployment in

Cambria County, women and men talked to each other out of their own experience and filled out questionnaires that asked about their needs. It was clear that certain needs were falling between the cracks of unemployment benefits, welfare checks, and even Operation Touch, the local arm of the Roman Catholic charity St. Vincent de Paul. These ranged from paper products to dealing with unshakable thoughts of suicide. In the meeting it was made clear that those who were facing mental depression were reluctant to seek help from professionals but would appreciate talking to others of their own class who were also unemployed. In spite of the well-organized services provided by Operation Touch, its compassionate staff of professonals and volunteers, and its well-intentioned administrator, John Sroka, the families of the unemployed felt as alienated from this "benevolent" agency as they did from government services. Alienation focused not on the performance of the agency so much as what it represented: seeking help from the upper classes, the "haves."

Of course, the "we/theyness" had always been part of Johnstown society and consciousness. But when one's ego was feeling especially bruised, going to Operation Touch could literally be adding insult to injury. The emotional cost was too high. When self-dignity is becoming a rare commodity, the last ounce of pride is preserved by fending for oneself. It was out of this shared need for collective self-development (rather than depending on the generosity of the professional-managerial class) that the Wives' Action Committee had its beginning—or, more appropriately, "its uprising." Mary Duranko, founder and president of the WAC, spoke about the development of her organization:

A steelworker is a proud person. These men have worked all their lives. It's opening up another world to them to tell them they have to live off charity. That's a hard lump to swallow for anyone who has supported a family. . . . These people are fighting together. They're uniting. We're trying to bring our families together —what we have lost. I think it's about time that Johnstown gets out there and fights back. . . . What we have going here is something we are doing as a family. If nothing else, we are going to save our dignity, and there isn't any agency in town that can give us that back.[3]

The Wives' Action Committee has developed an impressive number of services: food and clothing distribution, information and referral services, telephone peer counseling, an annual Christmas dinner for unemployed families, and a versatile Crisis Team, which responds as advocate and intervenor in a variety of situations. Although none of the volunteers are professional social workers, communications, record keeping, and service delivery are performed efficiently and, more importantly, with *compassion:* not compassion as in a feeling of sympathy, but in the identification of those who share a "common passion," a common suffering.

As the Wives' Action Committee gained momentum and visibility, those in the social service community became offended. They wanted to show sympathy, not be put on the defense by angry demands. They wanted to give charity, not hear cries and accusations of injustice from their clients. Interclass tensions, which were latent or at least manageable before, broke out in a war of words between the two helping agencies. Mary Duranko and John Sroka, representing two different approaches to the "who" and "how" of meeting basic human needs in times of crisis, were pitted against each other.

Sroka maintained that Operation Touch represented a centralized system for food distribution and that opening other food pantries would only serve to confuse both food donors and clients. He did not believe that steelworkers were reluctant to take their needs to a professional agency. Further, he thought that if the wives wanted to continue in their work, they should do it "through the system." He suggested that they abandon their food distribution or merge it with his food bank. Their volunteer counselors could operate out of his agency. Finally he complained that the WAC provided services *only* for steelworkers (thereby basing their distribution of services on a "right" and not a need). "It is an abuse of the system," he said, "and the needy are not being served—it's the *greedy.* "[4]

Duranko and the Wives' Action Committee saw their sincerity and legitimacy being called into question. Sroka was challenging their credibility in the community. They thought that the economic crisis in Johnstown did warrant another food pantry, and they did not see themselves as in competition with Operation Touch. They did not understand why the WAC seemed so offensive. What they did not fully comprehend was that their organization was unique, not only in its services but, more centrally, in its class identity and operating premises. Their major product was less tangible than a bag of groceries and more real: it was the dignity of self-help and self-expression. In spite of family hardship, the wives refused to be lumped together as "the needy"—those who depend upon the benevolence of the privileged classes. The purpose of their work was to help individuals protect their dignity and thus survive poverty as persons of self-respect. Their instrument was to cry out against the inequities and injustices of the economic crisis and to work together for survival and change.

John Sroka did not understand the nature of the conflict; to understand it he would have had to change his own class perspective. He was baffled that when his people went to WAC meetings they were "treated like the enemy."[5] He is well-respected in Johnstown; the sincerity of his intentions in helping the poor is generally unquestioned. The response he usually receives is one of gratitude and recognition.

Duranko recognizes the conflict without fully understanding it and just asks that the charity establishment allow the WAC to continue unimpeded. "It would make life so much easier if St. Vincent de Paul would just back away from us and let us try to do this. I don't understand why St. Vincent de Paul is attacking us. We are only trying to help ourselves."

As nonprofit agencies become necessarily more competitive in appealing to the finite pool of contributors, chances are that the charity war will intensify. The profoundly symbolic clash between the poor-but-proud underclass and the sympathetic-but-superior upper class will probably continue to be at least one of the stages on which brewing class tensions will be acted out.

The dread of losing middle-class status, of course, fuels one's interest in preserving it. When unemployment and underemployment hit across the class lines that used to define social standing, the cultural trappings may still hold things in place. "Helping those less fortunate" comes not only from altruism, it is also motivated by the less noble desire to reassure oneself that there *are* those who are worse off. Volunteering or contributing to a local charity is an investment in preserving the social stratification, as well as being a personal coping mechanism. The class structure, which in good times helps people define themselves in relation to one another, thereby separating neighbor from neighbor, is, ironically, reinforced rather than transcended during hard times.

A New Fatalism

When Johnstonians become philosophical about the meaning and workings of the world, it is clear that their understanding of the future of individuals and their community is shifting. Gone is the old worldview—brimming with its coherence and optimism. Somehow it was easier for people to believe in the Providence of God when they felt they had more control over their lives. With the economic disaster that has befallen this community, there is a third mark of the evolving culture: a new fatalism is setting in. Life just seems so random. Coal miner Harry Lloyd expresses it:

Right now, we're laid off with eleven, twelve years of experience in the mines. You sit back and wonder—y'know—What's life? It's just breaks. You know what I mean? You get the right break, you could be on top of the hill.

You don't get the right break, you're fightin'.

This fatalism is an extension of, though distinct from, the sense of victimization. Victimization is personalized, case-specific, and focused on the cause. It is present reality created by a past event. Fatalism, on the other hand, looks into the future with passive resignation. The victim can still protest and fight back. The fatalist silently receives whatever life might throw. Today in Johnstown, there is a growing feeling that a worker, a family, a community have very little to do with creating their own destiny.

The worldview that is becoming evident in the culture of Johnstown since the economic crisis is not a simple or sudden pessimism. In the transition from the old to the new culture, two worldviews are often expressed: a perspective on the "big picture" and then an outlook on one's own life and future. Many folks are able to maintain a grim and cynical view of the wider world together with a still-hopeful forecast for their own lives. This macro-pessimism and micro-optimism remain in a manageable tension for a while, as if one is saying, I think that nuclear war is inevitable, but I am planning on a long and happy life. But how long can the dual mindsets continue to coexist?

For Katie Ritchey, they were finally fused when she could no longer keep the economy from invading her personal reality. Disappointment swamped her life. Ritchey is the third generation to own and run the Maple Avenue Cafe in Johnstown, which through the years has fueled thousands of steelworkers with coffee and home baking. The first flood of the century leveled the family business. But they believed and rebuilt on the same spot. In 1977, violent waters again washed away the cafe, as well as the Ritcheys' home and two other houses they rented for extra income. But again, they believed in a future of growth and prosperity. Expecting that Bethlehem Steel would dig out and renovate the nearby factories, the Ritcheys borrowed $150,000 from the Small Business Administration and again rebuilt the cafe.

But now customers are few, for only a handful of employees still work in the once-booming steel plant. Filing for bankruptcy, Katie Richey at sixty is disillusioned and depressed. "I see myself as down-and-out. That hurts. . . . We can't live like this. We're worried and don't know what to do. This place is part of us. It's my mom and dad. We used to pack them in here every shift. We had them coming and going. Now we're down to nothing."[6] Katie Ritchey is experiencing the death of her dreams and, simultaneously, the death of her parents' dreams. In their place, the Ritcheys have aquiesced to the fatalistic expectation of random forces that now seem to have control over their lives. The micro-optimism to which they had clung has finally melded into their macro-pessimism.

In a culture of disappointment, a promise made together for the future is abruptly canceled—without counsel or consent. Disappointed dreams, like those of the Richeys, mean that hopes and promises between the generations are drastically changed. Parents cannot raise their children the way they had planned and taken for granted. They cannot pass on their good work. What they give instead are broken dreams. As a cultural heritage to carry into the future, their children receive a sense of powerlessness and fatalism.

This is the most profound level of injury of the new unemployment and underemployment—a new culture of disappointment, a culture of permanently lowered expectations in life, a fatalistic worldview. It is a grief and loss of the next generation which may not even be identified as grief or disappointment, just reality. The children and parents we interviewed in Johnstown spoke of a shadow that had passed over their future.

Shannon Gilroy figures that she would be twenty-eight years old in the year 2000. Her dreams were different from those of her mother at age twelve. Shannon dreamed not so much of a home and family as she did of becoming a doctor, although she quickly added, "I would take anything if I couldn't find a job." As a matter of fact, when asked what she thought she would be doing in A.D. 2000, she said, "Probably looking for work." The parent of another child said, sadly, that the only dream of her thirteen-year-old was "not to be on welfare." As the future builders of Johnstown, the young are being raised with shortsighted expectations and truncated dreams.

The powers that be in Johnstown—city administration, merchants, and bankers—struggle against this growing spirit of fatalism in their community. Against it they proclaim "the Johnstown Spirit." They have organized a campaign to change Johnstown's public (and self-) image. The hope is that by portraying their town as being extraordinary in its ability to pull together, think positively, and indeed triumph over such formidable obstacles as floods and plant closings, outside businesses will be attracted to Johnstown when considering relocation. For example, the local paper published a special "We're Proud" edition as part of the campaign. A full-color section was given over entirely to "good news" about Johnstown and its satellite communities in Cambria County. The author of the idea envisaged hundreds of copies of the edition being sent out to the Fortune 500 companies, to the President, and to members of the U.S. Congress and the national press.

One wonders what they hoped to accomplish. It's not as if Johnstown is the isolated victim of a new flood, ready for rescue. Today, there are hundreds of Johnstowns in the older industrial cities of the Northeast and upper Midwest. Knitting mills that fled to the South a hundred years ago are now being pushed out of business by even cheaper wages in Taiwan and China. Factories that built cars and made electric irons in southern California and Texas have watched that work cross over into the Export Zone on Mexico's northern border. These mobile industries have left a series of broken communities and transformed cultures in their wake. If Johnstown stood alone, it would be easy. It is when we realize that Johnstown is *symbolic* of much that is happening in the rest of the nation that we start to get a grasp on our new economic challenge.

One Pennsylvania State Representative (not from Cambria County) was led to comment, "Johnstown, and cities and neighborhoods like it, will never really be dead, although they'll always be dying." The question poses itself: Just how many "cities and neighborhoods" did the politician have in mind—could stand to have in mind? The culture which developed around the smoothly running mechanism of the American capitalist economy, the culture which in turn nurtured the national morale and contributed to its continuity, is beginning to unravel. Jobs are being permanently lost. New jobs being created are paying less. High technology and the service economy cannot begin to fill the void left when manufacturing jobs travel to the third world. The number and success of "yuppies" (young urban professionals) has been greatly overestimated. Of the demographic bulge created by the baby boomers (those 79 million Americans now between the ages of twenty and forty years), more than half are currently unemployed or earning less than $10,000 a year. Only 3.6 million are earning $35,000 or more—considered a respectable yuppie salary. The rest—approximately 35 million—are in the solidly lower-middle-income bracket of $10,000 to $35,000.[7]

As unemployment and underemployment cease to be temporary setbacks and are recognized as being permanent parts of the new national economy, as downward mobility becomes entrenched for so many, disappointment will become enculturated.

As we left Johnstown behind on the train traveling east, slowly climbing the mountain gorges of the Alleghenies and heading toward the famous Horseshoe Curve and, beyond that, to the great cities of the East Coast with their hospitals, educational institutions, and financial centers, it occurred to us that Johnstown—what it really means—still lay ahead of us, beyond the shallow scenarios of economic recovery, beyond the official optimism that leaves the present generation of victims of the economy feeling even more isolated and unworthy.

The American dream is in crisis—a crisis of its own making. If we are to understand that crisis, we must understand more fully what it means to become a member of "the new poor," to expect a future that hard work will slowly make better and better and then see that future turn into a nightmare.

3

Blue-collar Blues

"It was very good to me, the job," Tom Barrett said, "and it's times like this when people sit down and discuss what happened that I think about it, and it's not a happy thing to think about. I don't know what to compare it to. Maybe it's like the death of a friend, a good friend, or someone in the family. It's a very deep emotional thing, the loss of a job you've had so many years. You thought you had security, and it wasn't there."

How can we understand the experience of people like Tom Barrett, who have worked steadily for twenty or thirty years and suddenly find themselves without work, or have to go back to work at a third or a half less pay, or can find only part-time work? We can begin with our own experience. At a party where strangers meet we are asked again and again, "What do you do?" We answer, "I am —————." We identify ourselves to others in terms of our work. That is one reason why unemployment is so shattering, so confusing to the victims. Others continue to work and know who they are when asked, "What do you do?" But the unemployed only know who they were but are no longer. "I used to be a steelworker," they say.

That scares the rest of us. Like the lepers of biblical times, the unemployed and those whose lives have been radically redefined by underemployment have a disease for which our society knows no healing. They remind us of how precarious our own place in society is. "What would we talk about?" The friends of an unemployed steelworker ask, in explaining why they don't see their friend anymore. As if they were in grief, we leave the unemployed alone because we have no answer in our own lives for the pain we see in theirs.

But silence is the most terrible thing of all. It is a wound inflicted first by others who are afraid to see or hear. Then it deepens into a wound the self inflicts upon itself. The unemployed come to believe they have no right to protest, nothing to say that other people need to hear. Theologian Dorothee Soelle understands the danger of this self-silencing.

> The first step towards overcoming suffering is to find a language—that leads out of uncomprehended suffering that makes one mute, a language of lament, of crying, of pain, a language that at least says what the situation is.[1]

Like a death in the family, unemployment and the collapsing dreams caused by underemployment need grieving; people need to cry out. Pretending nothing's wrong, pretending things are getting better, leaves the victims not only alone but feeling guilty for their loss, unclean in a society of obligatory optimism.

Grief is something we usually think of as intensely personal. And indeed it is. But grief is also something public. It is a social phenomenon. How we understand our loss—the meaning of our pain—is always something learned. And society is our teacher. In this case our culture's understanding of work, and of the expected rewards for hard work, deeply conditions the way that the unemployed person experiences his or her loss.

The American dream establishes the framework for understanding work in our society. This is the notion that hard work and clean living will lead to a constantly better way of life, for ourselves and even more for our kids. Besides the mourning a worker goes through when he or she loses a job, there is a second experience of loss, a second period of grief when a new job is found that is so often at a significantly reduced wage and benefit level. Just when friends and relatives—indeed, the whole society—is saying, "Well, it's O.K. now; people are going back to work," the truth is that things are not at all O.K.; grief intensifies. Harvey Brenner, an epidemiologist at Johns Hopkins University, tells what it's like to have underemployment follow unemployment.

> As long as they were between jobs, between positions, it was possible to imagine that the recession would go away, that all the bad things—poor income, lowered self-esteem—would go away. They won't go away for many people, because what is left afterward is a lower position socioeconomically than they had before the recession. So what we have is a second period of grief. That loss will be permanent for these people. They will not regain their economic and social position for the remainder of their lives.[2]

The American dream made a different promise. A gift between the generations, a source of hope and of family solidarity, something everyone depended upon, is being taken away. Not just the unemployed but the downwardly mobile reemployed are in grief. And what they grieve is not simply the loss of a job, or a new job that's not as good. It is the loss of a whole way of making sense out of life.

Let's listen to those in grief—a private but even more a public grief, a grief with separate and distinct periods of expression. In listening the rest of us can hear, if we let ourselves, not those who are different, people we can put "over there" and feel sorry for. We will hear, instead, ourselves. And we will know ourselves better because we will have heard our own worst fears spoken aloud.

They once made good money, those steelworkers of Johnstown and the coal miners in dozens of small mining towns that hover around the mills and once fed the blast furnaces of the valley. Their children and their children's children followed them into the mills and mines, where work was hard but workers' pay was some of the best anywhere in America. That didn't come easily. Unions had a long and bitter and often violent fight. But eventually they won for their members a way of life that we call American. Today, that American way of life is dying, and the people are in grief. In their lament we hear echoing the cry of millions of our nation's industrial workers who are also unemployed, or underemployed, and on the skids.

Mary Duranko gives voice to what is in effect a liturgy of grief.

If I was his wife and he knew I was having a depression and I told him, "I'm mentally depressed, I need help," he's not going to admit it. Because he's going to have to carry that—"Well, I caused you to get in that position." So he says, "You're not going anywhere for help." Meanwhile, I'm going further and further into a depression.

O.K., so he goes out drinkin' in a bar to calm his feelings. He comes home. She says the wrong thing. They start fighting. And it gets worse—you've got abuse.

O.K., then you get a little kid sittin' on the steps that used to see Mommy and Daddy, you know, lovey-dovey. Now you hear Mommy yelling at Daddy, Daddy yelling at Mommy, hitting each other. And the kid can't understand it.

O.K., then the kid comes down the next day and asks you for a quarter 'cause he wants something. You can't give it to him. You tell him you can't afford it. Well, then the mother feels bad. She tells the dad, "Tell the kid you're laid off!"—You know, it's your fault.

So the kid hears all this. Then the kid starts going—"It's my fault. I got Mommy and Daddy fighting, and Daddy hit Mommy, 'cause I asked them for money." So then you got the child taking the blame.

So when the child goes to school, he's not thinking about the schoolwork. He's wondering, Is Daddy hitting' Mommy at home? Is Mommy really going to pack her bags and leave? Is Daddy really going to pack his bag and leave? Is there going to *be* a home?

Economically dependent women experience the unemployment of their husbands in a grief tailored by their situation, as we will see in the next chapter. For both spouses, however, it is a radical and devastating experience. Unemployment attacks the way people live together, often turning the family from a system of mutual shelter into a battlefield of accusation and anger. Mary explains:

I look at him and he looks at me, and I blame him. "Well you're not working and I have to work! Don't yell at me if the house is dirty or this or that. I can't afford to wash clothes because I don't have the detergent to wash clothes!" So he starts yelling at me, "Well, I'm sorry I ever married you!" and all this. You know: "I'm only staying with you 'cause of the kids."

Well, then, I figure, "Hey, I'm a human being too—why the hell am I stayin' married to you? You're not doing anything for me. You're not helping me. You're not helping my kids!" Hey, I'd love to pack up and just leave.

Job-related grief can undermine the most basic bonds. Loved ones become each other's tormentors, as each becomes for the other the symbol of their own entrapment.

Another result of long-term unemployment, a situation that often persists when the next job the husband gets is at a third or a half less pay, is role reversal. Men see the family having to depend on paychecks their wives bring home. They have lost their place as provider. They grieve over a lost identity. They are angry. Sometimes they blame the bosses and the company. Other times they blame their wives. Always they blame themselves and feel ashamed.

Harry Lloyd is a coal miner—or at least he was until Bethlehem closed down Mine No. 31. We are sitting in Clara Johnson's living room ten miles north of Johnstown in a mining town called Nanty Glo. Sitting around are a dozen other out-of-work miners and millhands, many with their wives. They talk about the dramatic change in their lives.

Harry Lloyd is barely able to keep his voice from breaking:

When both my kids were born, I got down on my knees and I thanked God for them. You know what I mean? I just wanted to make a living, for me and my family. And it's just . . . wiped out.

I went down to the unemployment office. Two more checks to come in! That's when you come home and you start takin' it out, maybe on your family. Watching' TV, your family layin' up in bed, and you're wonderin' what in hell you're gonna do to feed them. If you have any pride as a family man, it hurts.

His wife, Lyla, works in a sewing factory. About her work she says, "I don't make enough money; we couldn't live solely on my salary. But I make enough that we aren't eligible for food stamps, aren't eligible for medical aid. Sometimes you wonder, maybe you'd be better sittin' at home." Harry is now very excited. Unable to contain himself, he interrupts:

Like I said, you're watchin' TV at night, and your family's in bed, or she works and you're layin' in bed. She's gettin' up at five o'clock in the morning. The wind's blowing outside, and it's snowing. You wished you were goin' out that door. I houseclean. I help —y'know—I iron and keep the house up to help her out. But that's not my role in life. I'm the provider: supposed to be, anyway.

Clara Johnson tries to comfort: "But your kids are pulling for you, one hundred percent!"

Harry cuts her off. "But you shut that out because of your pride —you know, your own self-pride."

We come to prize ourselves because we see others needing us, depending upon us, because others—our family, our workplace— find us skilled and useful. Harry Lloyd is grieving a lost worthiness. He has lost his place in the family.

He has lost something more—his way of fitting into the wider society. Unlike other species, human beings have no built-in instinctual clock. We must construct time out of social conventions. In adult society, work is the major instrument by which a common clock is established. Going to work, coming home from work, weekends—these orchestrate and pace our time together and time apart. Without work to structure his time, Harry finds himself staying up into the early hours of the morning, watching television alone, and listening helplessly in the early morning when others leave to join a world he is excluded from. Unemployment means losing a way of putting your days together. It is personally and socially disorienting.

Tony Longo lives in a working-class neighborhood in Philadelphia. In the twenty-eight years of his life, he has never found steady work.

Unemployment gets you scared. You start studying yourself. Are you a person? Are you able to work? I used to start looking at the papers, and sometimes it would only be one sheet of jobs in the whole paper. There was nothing you could do. Sundays come and you look, and there's nothing you can do. It would be hundreds of jobs there, and there's nothing you can do.

So they sent me down to the welfare office after my unemployment ran out. They gave me money from welfare. So we're talking about a guy making $190 a week going down to $92 a week, then going down to $41 a week—and that's living? In America? How can you live on $164 a month? They want you to steal. They want me to be a criminal. They want me to go out there and bust somebody's face for money.

I used to work at the gas station where all the junkies would come and buy and shoot dope. It would stay right around Second Street. But then the war [in Vietnam] ended, and the depression got worse, and you could see the economy getting bad. The neighborhood went completely down. The junk came in, more and more junk—narcotics, heroin, sniffing glue, anything to get away. I was there. I used to want to get so much stuff. Like you try to get your mind away from where you're at.

It's easier for you to be dead than to take the hassle. It's easier to be high than take the hassle. I believe people shouldn't have to live if they don't want to. A lot of Americans aren't living. They're hoping, but not living. I don't want to be that way. They get you hoping. They put you in the factories. You get that house. You get that car. But you get very little for your labor. Some people get their dreams. They build their dreams. But most get trapped.[3]

The emotional turmoil caused by unemployment that Mary Duranko and Harry Lloyd and Tony Longo talk about is the depth dimension behind what shows up on the surface as shockingly increased health risks for those whose jobs have been displaced or who face long-term layoff. Evidence is widespread that job loss leads to increased rates of alcoholism[4] and of wife and child abuse,[5] increases in suicide[6] and in homicide,[7] and a rising incidence of heart attack and other symptoms of acute physical and mental distress,[8] including first-time admissions to mental hospitals and prisons.[9]

Specifically, Dr. Harvey Brenner of Johns Hopkins University, using sophisticated statistical techniques, projected, in terms of its mass effect, the mental and physical health results of job loss. For every 1 percent increase in sustained unemployment, Brenner's figures project 37,000 additional deaths, including 920 more suicides, 650 more homicides, and 500 more deaths due to cirrhosis of the liver. There are 7,000 additional admissions to state mental hospitals and 3,300 additional state prison confinements. With each 1 percent increase in sustained unemployment there is a 5 percent increase in the number of suicides and a 7.5 percent increase in homicides among young males between seventeen and twenty-four.[10]

Brenner's statistics take on new and startling meaning when we realize that over the past decade the problem of unemployment has gotten steadily worse, and so has the problem of underemployment. The Bureau of Labor Statistics indicates that unemployment reached a low point of 4 percent after the recession of 1975. After the recession in 1979, unemployment never got below 6 percent. And the recession of 1981–82 left behind an unemployment rate whose low point was 7.1 percent and has since gotten worse.[11] For those finding new work in the service economy, while manufacturing earnings averaged $369 per week in 1984, the average for service work was $248, more than 30 percent less.[12]

Some argue that these recent high rates of unemployment are only a temporary phenomenon. The long-range outlook for employment, they say, is far brighter. Once the baby-boom generation is past, fewer persons will be entering the labor force, and unemployment will drop sharply.[13] This may or may not prove to be true. But even if true, the problem of a downwardly mobile pattern of new-job creation will persist.

The closing of the Youngstown Sheet and Tube plant in January 1978 illustrates this—4,100 workers lost their jobs. Two years later, *Fortune* magazine did a follow-up on the workers. Of the original number unemployed, 35 percent had been forced into unwanted early retirement, with their income halved. Another 15 percent were still unemployed two years later, thereby getting dropped from unemployment compensation rolls and becoming part of the poverty statistics. The remaining 20 to 40 percent had taken drastic pay cuts in finding new work, a phenomenon known as skidding, or downward reemployment.[14]

Whether it be steel, automobiles, machine-tool production, coal mining, or manufacturing, the best-paying blue-collar jobs in our society remain in sharp decline. Steel output is down by nearly 30 percent since 1974. The machine-tool industry remains in deep crisis, with orders in 1984 half the 1979 volume and employment down 30 percent from the 1979 peak. Despite record profits in the auto industry, the combined effects of new technologies and over-time work mean that more than 100,000 workers remain laid off. Most of them will never get their jobs back.[15] Economist Barry Bluestone concludes:

The traditional industrial America is disappearing. We've seen that in the auto industry, in steel. We've seen it happening in some parts of the petrochemical industry, the tire industry. That was the part of America that was really responsible for what we call "mid-dle America." It was the set of industries that produced a higher standard of living for workers in this country than any set of indus-tries in our history. Now that's disappearing.[16]

Harvey Brenner has discovered that this new downwardly mobile pattern of jobs produces many of the same negative health effects for the workers involved as actually being out of work. In a June 1984 study prepared for the Joint Economic Committee of the U.S. Congress, Brenner demonstrated that a declining trend in incomes in 1973–74 correlated to a 3 percent increase in overall mortality, or nearly 60,000 deaths in excess of what would be regarded as normal. There was an increase of 45,000 deaths from cardiovascular causes, as well as increases in suicide and cirrhosis of the liver.

What Brenner's study demonstrates is that many of the same symptoms of family stress come back just when outsiders think the bad times are over: when the unemployed go back to work. But people going back to work at lower pay and benefits tell us that things are not all right! Consider what's happening to Jack and Lee Thomas.

Jack is thirty-seven years old, a Purple Heart veteran of Vietnam and the father of nine- and eleven-year-old sons. Twice in his work career he has had a plant pulled out from under him. Fourteen years, and he's back where he started.

Fourteen years—I have nothing to show for fourteen years. No pension, no seniority, no vacation time. Nothing! My best year was 1978, and if memory recalls me rightly I made just a little over $23,000. Right now [1983] my base pay is $14,000. You're looking at roughly $10,000 difference. That's a lot of change.

Jack went to work for the Nesbitt Company right out of high school. It had recently been acquired by the ITT Corporation, and he liked the idea of working for a big company because he thought it meant security.

I want a job where I can be somewhere forever. I mean I have friends and relatives who have years and years with the company. And the company helps them and they help the company.

But in 1972 ITT started moving work out of Philadelphia. Jack was lucky. He found work at equal pay almost immediately. Once again, it was for a company recently bought out by a multinational—Yale and Towne forklift truck now owned by Eaton Corporation of Cleveland, Ohio. Seven years later, when Eaton closed that plant and sent the work to Mexico and Japan, Jack found new work *only at sharply reduced pay.* Statistics show that he made the wrong wager. Family-owned businesses are *less* likely to move, while companies recently acquired by a multinational corporation have a far higher rate of plant closings.[17]

Downward mobility begins a period of second grief. The anger and the depression and the sense of being trapped come back. Lee Thomas grieves not for the economic loss so much as for what, emotionally, it has done to Jack and to their relationship:

Here he has almost fifteen years into companies, and both times he's lost any kind of retirement. You lose the friends you've been around. I think they go into a depression. They feel they've lost something, and they don't know how to get it back. Just like you would have a depression if you lost a member of your immediate family. This is an immediate family to them.

He's not happy. He's not making the money he used to make. It's his third job since he was laid off from Eaton in as many years. He still doesn't feel like he belongs there.

I think if he wasn't married and didn't have a family to support he wouldn't have taken the job. He would have looked elsewhere or maybe tried something new.

He doesn't seem to realize how bad it's becoming between us. He doesn't talk about it. It got so it seemed that he was blaming me and the children for him not being able to try something new. [Lee bites her lip . . . and then begins to cry.] I don't know. I don't know whether he resents me, whether he resents his whole life. It hurts when you don't have what you used to have. It hurts when you think you're going to lose it. There have been times this past year that I have thought about it [divorce]. And I've never done that before. And just thinking about it scares me.

A lot of times him and I'll start talking, and we'll start crying because we are scared. We know what we have, and we know what we can lose.

I expect it to get worse. Until he finds what he's looking for, until he finds something that means as much to him as I do—that he can feel he's accomplished something in life—he's going to have this depression.

Whether it's Harry Lloyd, who is unemployed, or Jack Thomas, who is underemployed, each feels disappointed with his life—caught in family obligations that make them feel trapped and angry . . . and then ashamed.

Even more than unemployment, the downwardly mobile pattern of new jobs raises the question of fairness. Unemployment always seems temporary. But underemployment brings home the reality of a permanently changed future. This new reality—the millions of workers who thought they were secure within the American dream and now find themselves shut out—shows itself in the changed faces of many working-class neighborhoods. Mayor Joseph Battle of Chester, Pennsylvania, explained to a reporter:

> What happens is a multiplier effect. When a major plant closes down, it impacts the job structure of the whole community. Mom-and-pop stores—luncheonettes, shoe stores, the corner drugstore—it's like a string of dominoes. First factory workers get hurt, and soon everybody begins to feel it.[18]

Located south of Philadelphia along the Delaware River, Chester was for generations a thriving industrial city of blue-collar neighborhoods clustered around churches, small shops, and parish schools. Today, Chester is one of the economically most distressed cities in the country. According to Mayor Battle,

> Since 1945 Chester has lost an average of 1,000 jobs a year. The problems here seem to be an advanced state of the same problems facing other older industrial cities—the flight of factory jobs that used to be the backbone of the local economy.
>
> We're in a double bind. Already we've had to let go city workers, including 25 police officers. We know that plant layoffs mean more crime, more drug and alcohol abuse, more family problems . . . more need for social services. But the city has a shrinking tax base. That means more problems and less money to deal with those problems—a real double bind! And Chester's not alone. A lot of places in this country are headed where we are.[19]

Neighborhoods follow paychecks . . . downhill. In Kensington, a Philadelphia blue-collar community, a young widowed mother of five remembers how growing up "on these same streets, summers we was always barefoot. Then they wasn't full of glass like now."

We are doing something very foolish in our society. We are allowing socially unrestricted capital mobility to tear the financial and cultural roots out of working-class neighborhoods. We are undermining the human meaning of work, undermining belief and trust in the work ethic.

We have seen, concretely, the costs to family and to community when managers of capital decide to close a factory, move work elsewhere, and leave behind people who are without jobs or who can find work only at lower pay. But we need to note that none of these costs appear as costs to capital. We keep two sets of books in our society. What shows up as profit for capital may register on the books of community as loss and injury. But because there are two sets of books, no one seems to be responsible. So we never get hold of our society as a whole—capital and community *together*.

We are at a crucial turning point in the life of our nation. The new global economy and the competition of third-world workers mean that we are rapidly becoming more divided as a society—with some still having good work but more and more having to work for low wages and few benefits. If we do not soon find a way to reverse this trend we shall poison the spirit of our nation. Bill McAffee sees this. He worked at Eaton for seventeen years, and while his new job is better than Jack Thomas's, it has nothing like the pay and benefits he had before. He complains. And then he makes an ominous prediction.

Who does the economy belong to? Who's supposed to benefit? They must think we're dumb.

Here's U.S. Steel that can't upgrade its plants and is screaming about dumping [of foreign steel]. And yet they can come up with $7.3 billion to buy an oil company. If they can come up with $7.3 billion for an oil company, they ought to be able to come up with the money to build modernized steel plants. Who the hell they foolin'?

One corporation after another is just runnin' around gobbling up everything. And it's really tax-break money. They're not puttin' money into producin' jobs.

People start losing 'cause the work's not there. I think it can get ugly. People know how it can be—how it was. It's not like during the Depression when we were poor to start off with and stayed poor. People *know* you can live good!

You're either gonna provide people with jobs so they can make their livings, and do for themselves and their family, or you're gonna start getting a real ugly society.

The ugly society that McAffee foresees is a society of privatized anger, with much need to blame—somebody, anybody, whatever satisfies.

Unfortunately, the American dream of individual opportunity open to all has never helped us see our society accurately. It encourages us to "dream up" in good times and "blame down" in bad. It stabilizes the status quo by deflecting anger from the system onto individual losers or onto scapegoat groups: women, Blacks, foreign competition. Meanwhile, the status quo remains amazingly unequal —at least for a nation that thinks of itself as democratic. The top 1 percent of our society owns 28 percent of all the wealth. And the top 20 percent owns an astonishing 80 percent of everything that can be personally owned.[20] With this kind of inequality, only rapid economic growth has made the American dream a believable promise, feeding the hearts and minds of the majority with a slowly improving life-style, while leaving unaltered the underlying division of wealth.

But then came the new economic realities of the 1970s and 1980s, with stiff international competition, the flight of U.S. capital to low-wage-rate countries, and the replacement of humans by machines. In response, politics have not become more liberal, nor have people become more kind. The American dream—that anybody can become somebody—does not serve us well as a guiding vision in a period of slow economic growth and a shrinking middle class. In hard times the dream invites self-blame rather than structural economic analysis. And in sustained hard times it encourages a disastrous distortion of conscience that finds satisfaction in taking it out on the poor while continuing to dream, forlornly, of someday—"if not me, then my kids"—making it to the top.

McAffee may be right about the new ugliness in America. But another laid-off worker sees a different future—a future where people begin to ask "What's fair?"—not just "How do I get mine?" That, too, has its roots in the American promise—a promise not just of a chance for personal success but of "a nation of the people, by the people, and for the people."

J.P. worked for Bethlehem Steel in Johnstown until his job was farmed out to a private contractor who paid minimum wage and no benefits. "We were conservatives," his wife says. "You know: work hard—save your money—don't spend unless you can afford—vote Republican." But after going through successive downgradings of job classification and finally permanent layoff, J.P. began to question. "Who did you get angry at?" we asked.

Who do I get angry at? I'm not particularly angry at anybody. I always was a very conservative person and a capitalist by nature. I understand the capitalist system, how it operated and how to be successful. And I always agreed with that system, until now.

It was great for this country when it was contained in this country. But this same capitalistic system now has no boundary lines. So they don't feel any social responsibility to the town or this country. The only thing they are interested in is profits. They don't care if lives are destroyed.

I don't feel that a handful of people should have the right to totally destroy communities. So I'm not the capitalist I thought I was.

As the new global economy begins to affect more and more blue-collar workers, perhaps many of them who started out thinking in much the same fashion as J.P. will come to the same conclusions. If so, the politics of the American labor movement could, for the first time, become radical in the sense of asking the question: Who should own and control work in our society? It is a question that many women in our society will also want to ask, because the new economic realities are affecting their work even more fundamentally than the work of men. We examine this in the next chapter.

4

Her Dream Undone

The unemployed beamed by TV into our homes often wear hard hats *and* neglected beards. That is to say, they are men. They bear the griefs that come from the loss of income, change in identity, and deterioration of hope discussed earlier. But the grief and psychic rearrangement that result from unemployment are not the exclusive domain of men. There are other faces, less often shown: faces of the wives and children of the providers who can no longer provide; faces of working women, some married, some single, whose own pink slip has meant much more than the loss of pin money. In many ways their experience of unemployment is similar to that of men, their grief shared. In other ways it is unique to women.

Clara Johnson, a miner's wife, remembers vividly the day her husband was laid off.

It was a day to remember, I'll tell ya. I kept telling him, "I heard these rumors. They're gonna close [the mine]." He says, "Never! They keep sayin' there's ten years left, there's twenty years left." I says, "Mick, there's rumors." He says, "Don't believe them." So . . . it came across the news. I went hysterical. Y'know, you figure you go from like a hundred dollars a day to—what was it then?— a hundred eighty-two a week on unemployment. I panicked. The whole bottom dropped out.

When the bottom drops out, the wives go through their own experience of grief. But their loss is different; their disillusionment is related to the illusion attached to growing up female in America.

The old values that worked so well for so long in All-American industrial cities like Johnstown were held in common by both men and women. But the American dream, with its promise for success, is premised on separate role expectations for women and men. The material content of the dream is the same: a nice home, a new car every few years, modest vacations, college education for the children, and hope for a little more of all of it for the next generation. But the means of achieving these goals are quite different for men and women. For men, the American dream is something to strive for, work toward, make happen. For women, it is something to be enjoyed. Males are raised with the understanding that their hard work will secure the dream. Women know that *their* labor (whether at home or on the job) will have very little effect on their dream's becoming a reality. As traditionally understood, the American dream is a *derivative* dream for a woman, contingent on the actions of a man.

Women have minimal control over the realization of their dream. In the mythology and traditional gender roles surrounding the American dream, they factor into the equation at only two points: in their initial judgment in choosing a husband and in their ability to continue to give him emotional support. If the American dream for men is about self-determination, for women it is about dependency. A certain alienation is therefore written into her dream and her work, if with invisible ink.

Born out of the Industrial Revolution, gender roles have been clear. While men participated in the production of goods, women were to be at work at home, reproducing the social order. For there to be a house, there must be a housekeeper. For there to be children of promise, there must be an at-home mother. For a man to be able to bear eight to ten hours a day sweating in the mill or eating dirt in the mines, there must be a hot meal, an easy chair, and an understanding woman at home waiting for him. Together they would keep the system going and keep their lives in balance.

When the dream is working out, it usually goes unquestioned in blue-collar families. Men and women play their parts and enjoy the anticipated results. But when *his* job is eliminated, unemployment dismantles the dream for women as much as it does for men. The immediate loss of financial security and a system of meaning is the first dimension of their experience of grief. When it looks as if the bank might foreclose on the mortgage and the house will be lost, when a woman who never thought she would have to work must find a job waitressing or cleaning someone else's house, when a wife must drastically cut back on necessities and cut out luxuries for her family, when a salary check has been replaced by an unemployment and then a welfare check—women experience a deep sense of betrayal. They feel betrayed by a tradition and a system that promised much and whose prescriptions they trustfully followed.

For the woman who has been financially dependent, the unemployment or underemployment of the man who supported her has a scatter-shot psychological effect. No area of her life is left untouched by the crisis. Everything is open to question. None of the cards are secure. Nothing looks quite the same—in her life or in the world. Questions that began as "When will Bethlehem Steel call him back?" become "What does it now mean to be an American? What does it mean to be a woman? What does it mean to believe in God?"

Mary Duranko chose to express her frustration and hope for change through organizing the Wives' Action Committee, as we saw in chapter 2. She described her response to some of her critics:

They'll say we're a radical group. Like, *my place is at home.* But yet they're the same ones that told me when I was young, you know, buy a home and settle down and take responsibility. Well, O.K., we did that. But now welfare owns my home. I can't have an insurance policy. I'm not allowed to have a funeral plot. I'm not allowed to have any of those things. So where's the responsibility? Who's right, them or me?

"They" had told Mary about the American dream. "They" had misguided her. "They" had betrayed her. And now "they" were criticizing her for speaking out of her pain.

Who do women blame? Who is this faceless "they" who deceived Mary and so many other working people? Sometimes it is the media, sometimes big business or the unions, sometimes the government, sometimes the culture that transmits the promises. But it is difficult to sustain such anger at the generic "they" who told women their place was at home. Eventually, the betrayal becomes focused on the one who was supposed to deliver the dream—the husband. Mary went through these feelings:

You know what it was like for me to have to go into welfare? I went into welfare, I *hated* my husband for two weeks. I *hated* him. I was gonna leave him. I was gonna take the kids and leave. To me, this [welfare] was unheard of. I mean, I came from a family where you paid your bills. There was eleven of us. We didn't have it easy, but we still made it.

Anger toward their men, as providers of the bread and providers of the dream, was almost universally expressed by wives of unemployed and underemployed miners and steelworkers in and around Johnstown. This is not to say that the wives were not understanding and sympathetic toward the men, who themselves were depressed and angry. However, there was still a need to blame *someone.* As women wake to the reality that their happiness and economic viability is contingent not on their own labor but on that of another, their anger toward their husbands is precipitated not so much by what the men have done or not done as by what they have come to represent.

Sitting in her carefully decorated Early American kitchen, Linda Gilroy appears to epitomize the female version of the American dream. At thirty-three, she is attractive and articulate. As her long painted nails tap out a background rhythm, she describes her up-bringing in Johnstown. Her father had left her mother and her to fend for themselves. Growing up in a public housing project, her head was filled with dreams. Linda's visions of her future were typical of the time and place, her ambitions intensified by her own history. She wanted to marry, have children, and manage a comfort-able home. Looking out the window on a crisp fall day, she watched her husband, Pat, daughter, Shannon, and dog, Terrie, playing in the large side yard. "Shannon has what I didn't have growing up—a doggie and a daddy." The trappings of her American dream had been in place: a home in Johnstown's suburbs, a loving family, financial security, and the ability to provide a little more for her child than she had had growing up. Until a few years ago, Linda's only worries were how to redecorate the living room, where to go for vacation, and a gnawing question in her mind about pursuing some sort of career. She was where she wanted to be.

Pat's disemployment did not happen suddenly but was more of an incremental phasing-out of his position at Bethlehem Steel over a period of three years. Through a series of layoffs, callbacks, trans-fers, and job reclassifications, he moved from making $25,000 per year in the mill to $15,000 in Bethlehem's security department, before finally being terminated.

Linda's dream was threatened, and her hopes for her family dimmed. She was hurt, angry, and felt betrayed. In spite of her obvious respect and affection for Pat, she too expressed ambiva-lence toward the one through whom the dream was to have been secured. She wrote in a personal letter to the authors:

> He was almost irrational about it. He was saying things like maybe I should divorce him now because he will only drag us down. . . . He is afraid I will leave him. God knows what is in my heart and I can't lie: there have been times when I felt toward him what must have been hatred, or close; complete betrayal. But to see him so shattered is heartbreaking. I tried to reassure him but I feel almost helpless. He needs more than I can give.

In that first dimension of grief over a dream lost, of asking how and why, of realizing the contingency of one's well-being, the bulk of a wife's emotional and physical energy still goes into the family. Paradoxically, she knows that when the dream dissolves (through her husband's or her own job loss or reduction), she will probably end up working harder. For married or even single women, a suddenly marginal family income means piecing together a patchwork schedule of low-paying part-time jobs—those most accessible to women—in addition to responsibilities at home.

This is quite different from the experience of unemployed men, whose major battles are not with the stress of overwork but with the anxiety of boredom. The woman is painfully aware that the responsibility for feeding, clothing, and holding together the family is still hers, although the tools and resources of her trade have changed. If jobs are unavailable, she must turn to charity and welfare, the two most offensive symbols to those who believed in the American dream. If there was a trace of one's dream left before, it is dashed when the unemployment benefits run out and a family must go on welfare. To stand in a welfare line for the first time is to grieve. For most of the families interviewed, it was the women who went out in search of material assistance. In their own shame and depression, the men refused to go. Wives of unemployed steelworkers commented on this at a meeting of Johnstown's Wives' Action Committee:

You can't better yourself if you're on welfare. You have to stay where you are, in a hole. See, they tell you to go get a job. But they want you to take a peanut job. They want you to take a job that you still have to depend on them.

Everybody that says that welfare ain't that bad. Well, tell them to live on it for a while!

[At the welfare office] you feel like you're going and you're taking from them. That's how they make you feel, that you're taking their bread and butter outa their mouths. Then they ask you all these questions. . . . They really downgrade you.

As they see their dreams eroding—dreams of being in the middle class, where the lack of a job outside the home is a mark of success —as they transfer their dependence to the faceless provider of state welfare, the wives of unemployed workers move into a second dimension of grief. They become aware of their utter vulnerability, their dependency, not just on their husbands but on outside forces beyond their control. Realizing their future will be determined by entities like "the politicians," "the union bosses," and (more realistically) the board members of multinational corporations, their eyes see beyond their immediate grief. They confront, for the first time, their own powerlessness. Their alienation from the system goes one level deeper than that of their husbands. Through unemployment they are not only denied participation in the economic world (their husbands' loss) but they also realize that they never had any real participation to begin with. The second dimension of grief for the wives is not the loss of power but the loss of illusion. When the grief surfaces, it does so as a deep rage to which the women are unaccustomed.

The Wives' Action Committee regularly demonstrated at the gates of Bethlehem Steel and took busloads of women to lobby in Washington. Mary Duranko herself became a well-known spokeswoman for the families of unemployed steelworkers, often appearing on local news programs and occasionally on national television. But her eloquent and graphic expressions of frustration often made her audience uncomfortable (a dynamic previously addressed). Mary believed that the negative reception she received from those not used to hearing women publicly express their anger at the "powers that be" was because she dared to tell the truth.

I don't beat around the bush. I will say exactly what [the problem] is. I mean, I don't believe in lying. Like when we went on that one television show, I told them, I says, "Hey, if you think I'm gonna lie, you're crazy! I am gonna say exactly what I feel and the way I see it". . . . They [the media] do not want everybody to know how bad Johnstown really is.

As her dreams and her worldview are lost, there is a third dimension of grief for the wife of the unemployed or underemployed worker. With the change not only in the family finances but also her husband's own perception of himself as a human-being-in-the-world, the wife's self-identity becomes the arena for loss and grief. Since much of the female identity has been constructed in the industrial society *in relation to* that of the working man, that too is open to question. Ever since women were "liberated" from the factories to the sphere of full-time domestic labor, wives inherited unambiguous gender roles in the ordering of everyday life. But now, traditional women in the deteriorating industrial cities of North America are experiencing a confusion and grief about themselves, perpetrated not by "women's lib" but by their husbands' unemployment and underemployment.

One laid-off steelworker's wife talked about how her marriage had changed:

I don't feel like I'm my husband's wife. I mean, right now I lost that closeness. I used to relax with my husband on the couch every night. That was our standard policy, 'cause I thought, you know, let your children see the closeness between Mother and Dad. Well, now if my husband comes near me, it's tension. Get away from me! I don't want it! I don't want his closeness. I resent it. It's a physical thing and that's it. He's not feelin' like a man anymore, so I feel less than a woman. Let's face it, you're often tempted to go out elsewhere just to recapture that one feeling that you had with your husband.

During a personal employment crisis, impotence is not uncommon among men. With greatly reduced earning power, they feel they can no longer fulfill the traditional male role. This can trigger confusion for the woman about her own sexual identity. In bed, there are the mixed feelings of resentment toward one another and personal injury. At a time in their lives when sexual intimacy could be a source of communication, support, and healing, it is often the focus of even further personal pain and alienation.

As part of the upheaval in one's sexual identity during this time, we found that for many women there was a change in perception from seeing their husbands as partners in building the dream to being children they needed to care for. The woman just quoted described this change:

In those three years [of her husband's unemployment], I learned to love him—and this is a terrible thing to say, but it's true—I learned to love him as my own children, because that's the way I looked after him, as a child. And basically that's my feeling toward him. If he got hurt, I'd be there to bandage it. Sleep with him? Forget it. I mean, you just . . . if you're forced to sleeping with your husband, for some reason, it seems perverted. Because you just don't know if it's your child or what. Because you just reacted to three years of this baby-sitting him. He became your child. And that's how you see him now. You do not see him as a man.

Her husband had been called back to the mill and was again supporting the family financially. But the change in the sexual arrangement had gone on for too long. What had begun as a temporary economic hardship had permanently altered their lives at the most basic level: their perceptions of themselves and of each other as husband and wife. Six months after the interview they filed for divorce.

Another component of the sexual identity of women indigenous to the American dream is that of emotional caretaker of the family. It is her role to dry the tears, bandage the scraped elbows, and patch the wounds. This one-sided responsibility continues in the employment crisis. But often, wives cannot break through the silence into which their husbands recede. His mute suffering frustrates her attempt to share in his grief and only multiplies her own. Sandy finally left her unemployed husband at the point when both were in pain but he could not find words for it. She could no longer tolerate the silence.

He just didn't realize just how bad *I* was taking it, and he wouldn't talk about it. He never sat down with me and discussed anything. How the bills was fallin' behind, he never knew that. He never looked at the mail. He never looked at the checkbook. [When I tried to talk to him] he would just get up and walk out. He didn't want to hear about it. . . . He didn't want to talk to me. I think he realized what was going on, but he just didn't want to face it.

This illustrates an important distinction in the way that men and women experience the grief of unemployment and downward reemployment. It is in their capacity or willingness to let grief find expression. The disappointment, disillusionment, and confusion carried by the husbands often gets no closer than a lump in the throat to being verbalized. Men can spend hours discussing the external realities of the situation—union politics, management promises, rumors and second-guesses of the future economy. But their background taught them no language for the devastation of a work-oriented identity; it was not considered necessary. As long as they worked hard and followed the rules, they would never feel like a failure, much less need to talk about it.

Women, on the other hand (as evidenced in Johnstown), are taught a vocabulary of internal realities. On the whole, they were able to speak much more readily to us about psychological pain, anxiety, love, depression, sexuality, conflict, and even suicide. Their need to articulate the turmoil boiling inside them contrasts sharply with their husbands' silence. Kim lamented to her friend, Mary Louise:

When you're down and out, they [the husbands] say things is gonna get better. Well, *when* are they gonna get better? You're depressed, you're crying, all that stuff, and he says, "Well, what are you cryin' about? There's nothin' to cry about." He don't know how I feel.

Mary Louise:

He's probably cryin' too, but he just don't let it out.

The affective perceptions and language of the women had been part of their socialization as females; they had learned and practiced it from childhood to adulthood in the context of their own social network and subculture. Injured, even as the men were, they were not left mute. They had been given social permission to cry out and express their pain. While their husbands found that their own network had been lost as part of the high cost of unemployment, the housewives' social circle remained intact, allowing them to find support during the boom and bust of the economy. Their socializing was affected somewhat by their husbands' unemployment. Tighter budgets preempted shopping trips or lunches out. With men spending more time at home, the privacy of morning conversations over coffee with friends was significantly limited. Cutbacks in community programs such as the YWCA in Johnstown eliminated recreational and educational programs that had served as important social contacts for women. Nevertheless, the women stayed in touch with each other. Girlfriends continued to provide an important emotional outlet, functioning as peer therapists as each helped the other survive poverty, their husbands' depression, and their own broken hopes.

Although grieving the loss of their dream, the new awareness of their powerlessness, and conflicts in their sexual identities, grief for these women was not paralyzing. Through their natural resources of language and social networks, they discovered that grief could be mobilizing.

The Wives' Action Committee is one manifestation of this possibility. There were about 25 women and a few men at their first meeting. Eventually, it was not unusual for 200-plus folks to attend the monthly meetings. And there was an interesting and unexpected development as women took leadership and expanded their vision of their work sphere. President Mary Duranko spoke of it:

We [wives] started it. We never anticipated the men, y'know, participating in it. It was basically going to be just for the wives to get together and get their anger out. Well, we got shocked when we seen the men! And now, it's one-to-one, I would say. And what's really great about it is the husband and wife both come together. She is so happy that he is taking it out up there [at the meetings] and not at her at home. And that means a great deal.

The male and female members of the Wives' Action Committee have seen their old gender roles fall by the wayside in their organization. In the process they have found a new partnership, based on a shared and vocal grief and the acquisition of new skills. It was the former male steelworkers who donned the aprons and prepared a turkey dinner for 800 families of unemployed workers at Christmastime. Women organized the event, negotiated food and toy donations, and emceed the program. This partnership represents a changing understanding of work by both women and men.

When the social symbol of validation—the paycheck—is removed or greatly reduced, a workingman must find other sources of dignity. He must walk in his wife's shoes, share in her labor at home, and justify to himself the meaning of work that is not rewarded monetarily. Nancy Bango's husband was laid off from the steel mills in Johnstown for three years. She too dealt with the silencing effect of unemployment, her husband's depression, and increased tensions in a family which most often describes itself as "close." Yet she also recognized the leveling effect that an economic crisis can have between men and women:

I think we understand each other a little bit better. He realizes that housework is a big bug for me; I can't stand it. I think I can understand his feeling better and maybe put myself in his position, and think what it would be like to go and look for a job and somebody tell you "You're too old," or "We're not taking applications," when they are. , . . I don't know. Generally, I just think we maybe respect each other more.

This is not to romanticize unemployment as a character-building experience or as a desirable means of women's liberation. Unemployment and underemployment of men in the industrial cities of the Northeast and Midwest have wreaked havoc in families and created social and internal turmoil for the wives. A woman's personal dreams are shattered, as are her dreams for the children. College, a professional career, and a comfortable middle-class lifestyle now seem as much of a lost hope for the next generation as they are for herself. She grieves for the past, the present, and the future. How could traditions, roles, and expectations that had promised so much actually deliver so little?

But what of those women who are working for pay, outside the home? How different is their experience when they lose their jobs?

Vannie is a woman whose reputation precedes her: "Just wait till you meet Vannie!" the miners' wives would say. She is somewhat of a heroine in Nanty Glo and one of the few blacks in the mining towns around Johnstown. Petite, feminine, and carefully dressed, a certain charisma is generated through her bright eyes and energetic gesturing. Vannie had worked as a housewife for several years. After her divorce, she had two children to support, so she entered the job market. She worked three jobs in traditional settings for female workers and earned traditional women's wages. But she wasn't happy.

I'm the type of person, I can't sit still that long. I had that job in the sewing factory, and I'd get eight, nine hours sleep a night and I'd *still* fall asleep at that sewing machine! It just bored me no end. The bartending job was O.K., but it just didn't pay enough, and it was too many hours.

Mining was in her blood. Her family life growing up revolved around the mining schedules of her father, brothers, and uncles. Eventually this work claimed the lives of her father (through black lung disease) and a brother (through an accident in the mines). At that point she was drawn, out of curiosity at first, to the mines.

I always wondered, what's so fascinating, all these guys are going underground. Then my brother got killed up at [Mine No.] Thirty-three a few years ago, and that's what really did it. I wanted to find out just what it was under there that, y'know, drove people underground. Why?

Well, then I found out: it was the money. It's not a bad job. The money's there. That's the main reason I think any female would go underground. I can remember the first paycheck I got from Bethlehem. It was a full two-week pay, and it was like over eight hundred dollars, clear money. To me, that was like bein' rich after working like sixty hours a week being a bartender or in the sewing factory.

Vannie has met with sexual harassment and sexism on the job but has been emboldened in confronting them, partly because of the position of the United Mine Workers union on equity. She even scheduled her second wedding on Mitchell Day (a holiday that commemorates the institution of the 40-hour workweek for miners.) She has the enthusiastic support of her husband and children (who wear

T-shirts announcing *My mom's a coal miner!*). Speaking of her husband, she said:

> We get along great. We did from the first time we met. He'd tell ya he thought he was marryin' a rich coal miner! Before we got married we lived together for a while and he was unemployed. So he took over the complete control of the house. I mean, the washing, all the cooking, cleaning, the whole nine yards, while *I* went out and made the living, till he finally found a job. And he was real good at it. I mean, it was like reversin' roles. And I was happy to see somebody do it. He kept askin' me, what did I want in a husband? And I says, "Somebody that knows how to cook and keep my minin' clothes and my bucket clean." And he says, "You found him!" So—we got married.

As real as Vannie's work satisfactions are, so are her fears of losing that work. Women mine and mill workers are being laid off too: in fact, disproportionately so, because of their lack of seniority.

What Vannie fears and dreads became for Rose Smrzlich a nightmare reality. As principal breadwinner, she is a thirty-year-old divorced mother of two who was laid off from her job in the steel mill in September 1979. "Because of a lazy husband," she had begun working in 1974. "My husband was always on S.I.P. [Social Insurance Program]. He was a drug addict. So then I went to the mills. He liked it. I paid all the bills."

Rose, an attractive and obviously fit woman, had to prove herself to the men in the mill in order to gain their respect and be able to work the more difficult but higher-paying jobs. She described the job as a "heater" that she assumed—working with heavy machinery and in constant exposure to high temperatures.

> I was workin' on Twenty-two and five heaters passed out. They were all guys, so they called me in. It was real hot that day. Brang me up from Twenty-two to Thirteen and told me, "Go heat on the track for J.P."—he was the one down there then. He [J.P.] looked at the white hat [supervisor] and he looked at me and he said, "I don't want that goddamned woman. Get her the hell outa here!" That's just what he said. And the white hat said, "That's it. She's the only one we got"—'cause I could go right in. I knew what to do. So when we got to the end of the car, I hit him five times in the leg with a rivet! [Laughs softly, but with pride.] After that, he come out, he told me, "Y'know what you did?" "Yeah, I know what I did. If you don't want it somewhere else, you better keep your

damn mouth shut!" After that, they *asked* for me as a heater all the time.

Rose was obviously proud of her work. After finishing an eight-hour shift, she would go to a second part-time job in a department store in order to support her family. "I was a worker: a mother, a housekeeper, a worker." She felt good about herself in those days, but not now. In the past five years of unemployment, her marriage broke up. Unemployment benefits ran out, and she now receives welfare. She has been frustrated in her attempts to find even part-time minimum-wage work.

I was goin' down to Unemployment every week, and I got yelled at by the guy behind the counter. Told me I had no business comin' down every week. Once a month, that's what he said. I told him, "When you put a sign up there that says that I can only come down here once a month, then I'll only come once a month." He told me I'm not gonna get a job unless I know somebody. That was his exact words. He said, "If you don't know nobody, you're not gonna get a job." He said, "You're wastin' your time comin' down here."

Rose has now been unemployed for as long as she was working in the mill. For the five years of her career as a heater at Bethlehem Steel, she earned over $16,000 a year (plus her part-time wages)—a modest income for a family of three, just inching them into the middle class. Since she has been on welfare, Rose's family receives approximately $5,600 a year, including food stamps. Her family used to eat out in restaurants occasionally. Last year, they had to eat their pet rabbit. Rose has stopped thinking of herself as productive and independent ("I *was* a worker," she says); she has started seeing herself as part of the new dependent poor. She feels trapped and powerless in her new self-identity.

For women such as Rose and Vannie, the American dream was not mediated through the employment of another. They shared the satisfaction of their male colleagues in having their work rewarded and validated through fair wages, in the ability to support a family, and in the possibility of dreaming even bigger dreams for their children growing up in the Land of Opportunity. But now Rose despairs that those dreams and satisfactions are irretrievably lost in the trap of welfare and the cycle of poverty. She cannot contribute, through wage labor, to the common good—or even to her family's good. She feels stuck.

I think it's worse for women. It affects you more. Like me. I have cousins that worked in the mills. Now their wives are out working and they're staying home baby-sitting. I don't have nobody to sit and watch my kids. It's harder for me, even if I would get a job. I gotta worry about—well, not so much my thirteen-year-old son but my four-year-old daughter. There's no way out of this rut. My caseworker told me, "It's unfair, Rose. The only thing I can tell you is to keep after your Congressman."

In spite of her skills and motivation to work, Rose probably is stuck for a long while. Recent research has shown that women are unemployed for longer periods of time and are reemployed at even greater wage cuts than men.[1] Part of the problem for unemployed women seeking new jobs is that they simply have fewer options. If they were fortunate enough to have made wages comparable to their male counterparts, their expectations were unrealistically raised. Upon reentering the job market, they find themselves herded into the ghettoes of "women's work," primarily in the service sector.

The anxiety and feelings of insecurity that are created by unemployment and underemployment are more persistent in those most vulnerable in today's job market—that is, women and minorities.[2] These people come to believe that the fleeting security they had when they were fully employed was a fluke. They cannot *expect* to be fully employed in their productive years in the way that white males have come to expect—and continue to expect, hanging onto the hope even during periods of unemployment and underemployment.

The employment crisis hits women hard. Whether working at home or in the job market themselves, they had breathed deeply of the American dream, only to have the wind knocked out of them. They were left reeling and confused. As the painful inequalities of women's work (paid and unpaid) bore in upon them, these women began to learn the realities of being female and in the working class —realities our official view of ourselves, our stated public values, do much to obscure and deny.

If we are to come to any resolution of the problems of the unemployed and the underemployed, we must look at these values more carefully—the myths, the realities, and the contradictions within which we try to make sense out of our lives. In the next several chapters we will examine this set of social values, within which work takes on its specific meaning in our culture. For the problem of work is not at heart economic, and its solution is not technical but ethical.

5

The Realities
of Social Class

We are told that we are a "middle-class society" that enjoys "opportunity for all," a society where everybody—or almost everybody—gets a chance at life.

That we are a middle-class society tells us that no one is locked in and no one locked out of opportunity because of their class origin. It tells us that there is a vast and mobile middle group in our society, which gives those at the bottom a chance to move up; while those at the top, without discipline and effort, can lose their position to more talented and motivated newcomers. That there is opportunity for all tells us there is hope for each of us to find our way to success. At the same time as keeping up hope, the idea of opportunity for all tells us that if we fail it is because we have not tried hard enough. Our life stories become individualized. Both the hoped-for triumph and the dreaded humiliation are in our own hands.

The idea that we are a middle-class society with opportunity for all says that those who *have* deserve what they have and those who *have not* just need to try harder. This has much to do with why our society so insistently looks at itself *from above*. What, we wonder, could those below us in society have to tell us? Except what we should avoid: pity . . . and, profoundly, fear.

Television is a perfect example of how our society looks at itself from above. Those who make the news are mostly those who have succeeded extraordinarily at becoming somebody: presidents, physicians, sports and entertainment celebrities. The exception is criminals and victims (of violence or bad luck). But it is not just the people we see. On the same television news we see products, usually of moderate price—soaps, toothpastes, appliances—placed in kitchens and bathrooms that are exceedingly expensive. The car we are urged to buy, even if quite average, is proclaimed to be anything but average and is shown sitting outside a house that is two or three times more expensive than the average person can afford. Whether it be popular social explanations, or those deemed newsworthy by television and newspapers, or the presentation of consumer products, we are inundated every day with society's "view from above."

That is why the view *from below* is potentially so intriguing. It is not simply that it is surprising—a voice, so to speak, out of the silence. Rather, the perspective from below upon a society used to seeing and interpreting itself from above can reveal a whole new way of seeing ourselves—a very disturbing way of seeing ourselves, given our usual self-understanding. The view from below contradicts the view from above and shows how the established explanations function to legitimate privilege and turn anger at society into self-blame.[1]

Usually, the view from below is unheard because people feel humiliated and think they have nothing to say that others need to know. But when men and women who are unemployed or underemployed protest and grieve aloud over their loss, it is like the sound of thunder, shaking the walls of society, because it unmasks society's myths and its institutions of legitimation.

Tony Longo grew up rock-bottom poor in Kensington, a working-class neighborhood of Philadelphia. He dropped out of high school in eleventh grade and is today functionally illiterate. His father never made it out of the marginal working class, and neither will Tony. Tony thinks he's dumb. He thinks he has nothing to say.

There was no education. I was supposed to take my father's job [as a machine operator]. Only they didn't have the guts to tell me. Why did they bother sending me to school? Shit, they should've just put me out to work when I was eight or ten! It was a false promise.

School was such . . . a rejection. I wanted to be with my friends. But I couldn't stay in school because I didn't have the tools. And it was always challenges that I couldn't meet. I'm sure I wasn't the only person with this kind of problem. The teachers, the administration—they knew we were going to drop out. We had to. I don't feel I dropped out: I was forced out of the system, which is a tracking system. I don't think it was a personal thing. It was just that they had so much of this one product, and the rest had to flunk out.

In school Tony learned that a "classroom" is very accurately named. It is a room where you learn your class.

I failed in high school. They let me go through junior high. It was a breeze. They knew; I'm sure they knew. My learning stopped in third grade, but they pushed me through. I thought it was the coolest thing that ever happened. This is where the family structure is really important. My parents should have known. But my parents were ignorant. So that's the pattern. I was supposed to take my father's job.

Tony sensed that his life was getting fundamentally bogged down, that quietly, with nobody saying anything, he was getting stuck.

But being dumb, being ignorant—it started catching up with me, and I started rebelling. Something was wrong! I didn't go out of my way to be a wise guy. But this attitude just started happening. I started getting smart with teachers, and they started suspending me—telling me to go home, bring my mother back in two days. My mother would come back with me, and that afternoon I'd get in trouble again. They'd tell me to go home for like two weeks. I couldn't believe it. It was like speeding tickets or something. You don't want to get them. You don't go out of your way to get them. But the guy's always there. So they told me to go to Edison High. Edison was ninety-five percent black, a really bad high school for white people. They were racists. I was racist. I went there for about a day, and then I said, "Forget this!" I dropped out of high school.

For people like Tony, school is an alien and alienating institution in the community. It doesn't reward the neighborhood: it mostly rewards those who want to get out of the neighborhood. It turns kids in the community into those who have to do battle with each other to find out who the few "talented" are. Somehow, the majority of the kids in working-class schools find out they don't have much talent. Many drop out; only a few go on to finish college.

It was the neighborhood, not the schools, that offered Tony support and shelter.

Yeah, the neighborhood was poor, but it was rich in people, richer than many other neighborhoods. It was like a town where everyone knew everybody—the stores, the streets. People used to help us out. Sometimes my father, his place used to go out on strike, and we didn't have anything to eat. So the neighbors would just pile stuff on our doorstep in the evening. There'd be boxes out there in the morning. It was more like a little town.

Only a few people on the block were working-class level and had that kind of income. Most people, if they made it to working-class standards, they thought they were middle class. My family was poor, sub-working class, which most Americans can't even imagine. They think it's Appalachia. We had four children, which was average if not small at the time. I think my father was making like eighty bucks a week. My father worked for a vinyl company for thirty-eight years. He was a machine operator—unskilled, very low pay.

He was only making eighty dollars! I mean, I think my first job I was making more than my father. That bummed me out. Like we were sitting around drinking some beer, and we started talking about work. He told me how much he made and I said, "Oh, my God! And I just *started* this job." It hurt to say it, but I feel it was good for him to know. Because I think he should start saving money as much as he can. They want to shut his place down because vinyl chloride causes cancer. A guy where my father works died of cancer.

I believe my father has something. He sounds like a coal miner, very bad cough. He looks beat. He is beat! There's nothing left, no mind. They really spaced him out. He has very little control. It sounds weird, but once you're broke for so long, and you're going to work with just carfare, you want to get free of it! So you take it out on the people you're around that usually love you. You get so pissed off, you don't look ahead. You don't see what's really happening.

Tony's view of neighborhood as shelter is widely shared among the urban working class. The shelter it provides is fundamentally a recognition of dignity and deservedness denied in the wider society. It is a value system that resists competitive individualism—the environment, for example, of schools. When a working-class person says "I'm nothing special," this is not a confession of low self-esteem but an estimate of self-worth not based upon "standing out from others."[2] It is an identity connected more to friends and to community than to individual achievement.

Working-class people are often perfectly aware of how class functions to humiliate those who refuse to stand out and "become somebody." They defend themselves and each other against this by a value system based upon "hard work" and "community pride." That is why taking work out of working-class communities is so unfair. It takes away not just paychecks but something far more important. It takes away the means of defending dignity. It attacks the workers' values that support their community and their personal identity. the theory of market capitalism knows nothing about this.

It does not even see what it destroys. What working folks value, the market does not value.

Tony's grasp upon class is brilliant. In his recollection that "if they made it to working-class standards, they thought they were middle class," Tony says in one sentence more about working-class voting patterns than many textbooks used in colleges. And his description of the "sub-working class" is equally insightful. His humiliation over his dad's low pay, the daily degradation of poverty ("going to work with just carfare"), and the anger that flares up at loved ones opens up the whole tragedy of family life in the underclass, where many times people who don't believe in their own worth raise kids with mixed emotional signals, confusing the kids and making them feel inferior. The result? The underclass reproduces not only itself but its relationships to other classes in society: "My parents should have known. But they were ignorant. So that's the pattern. I was supposed to take my father's job."[3]

There were limits to the friendship Tony's neighborhood offered, the limits of sameness. And there were limits to the safety and shelter it provided because the "officials" of society—the teachers, the police, the law courts—already had infiltrated the neighborhood.

What happened at one point in my life was I was rejected; my own people rejected me in Kensington. It was really rough for me to get around for a couple of years. It was 1969. I was into the counterculture. Not too many guys in Kensington had long hair or had black friends. And I had a really rough time with people that knew me; people I grew up with hated me overnight.

It may sound like nothing, but I was going through changes that to me meant a turn. I was around people that asked questions. I was around people that were challenging, all kinds of challenges: Where were they? Where were they going? For me that was dynamite.

I thought I was becoming an adult. I was supporting myself, illegal; but I was supporting myself. Then I got arrested for selling marijuana. The arrest was the thing that really brought the light. I found out that a poor guy shouldn't break the law because you're at their mercy. The police beat me really bad. They said I was lying about my age. They thought I was older than sixteen. They said I was eighteen. I had no ID. So they started getting rough. Like I said, at the time I was into a stage where I started getting wise. After they started hitting me a couple of times, I told them it didn't hurt, that I got hit by girls harder. And the punches started just coming and coming. They beat me all in my face and my head and my back.

My father came up to see me. They told my father I fell. They arrested me and beat me, and they covered it all up.

I got arrested with people that had money. They were getting out. I was there first, but I was the last one to go. I didn't get home for two days. That meant to me a poor guy shouldn't break the law. Because if he breaks the law and is poor, he's at the mercy of the law. Other kids' parents came up. They were educated people. The police didn't give them any hassle. But my father gets there, he's a working guy, with working clothes on, and they give this guy a hassle. And I was the only one that got beat up. Nobody else got messed with.

The police tried to brainwash me by keeping me awake. I smoked two packs of cigarettes in an hour. They beat me; they fed me cigarettes and coffee—no food. The clothes were ripped off my back. I was bleeding. All they wanted to talk about was, "Get a haircut, buy khakis and sneakers, get a job." No education. Just "Get a job and be a regular guy." They tried to pound it into me —physically. "Promise me you'll get a haircut!" By this time they were *pulling* my hair. After I left the police I had to go to the hospital. They said I fell.

That was the first time I really noticed how young I was. I never had a chance to be young.

By sixteen Tony Longo was already deeply enmeshed in the structures of class control, the ubiquitous "they" of his conversation: the schools, the legal system, the system of sub-working-class pay. The view from below came down early ("I never had a chance to be young"); and it came down hard ("I was supposed to take my father's job"). Society's institutions belonged to others. And they were not his friend. "They" were there to keep him in his place.

People like Tony battle to get in. But mostly they end up doing battle with those who share their own condition, others who are stuck at the bottom of our society and can't find a way out.

I remember this black family tried to move into a white neighborhood in Kensington. The first night the black people moved into the house, the house was filled with trash. All the windows were broken. The people still moved in. The police had to protect them, had to set up barricades. By the second night there must have been thousands of people surrounding the whole block. The police were trying to restrain them, but they couldn't restrain anybody. Rocks were thrown. There were groups of guys driving around in blackface, nooses around their necks. People that you'd never think would act like this. The younger people you expected it. But when you see older people start yelling "nigger this" and "nigger that," it got to be real.

One Sunday I saw this black kid get firebombed. A lot of white people had come into the area because they were curious. There were white people with dogs, waiting, ready. First the black man rode by in his car, and they hit the car with trash. I was just out of the matinee and walking down the street. A group of guys were on the corner, really angry. A black kid came out of Kensington Avenue, made a left down the street on a bike. He seen all these people with dogs and stuff and tried to make a U-turn and get out. As he turned somebody threw a Molotov cocktail. It hit behind the bike, but the gasoline shot up the guy's back. It was bad. The guy was screaming, rolling in the street. It was like a war. It was a real war, with hate! People wanted to kill.

The next day, Monday, the whole black community started coming over into Kensington. That's when war started happening. I remember hundreds and hundreds of black people were running out in the street. I was standing on the corner, really scared. We tried running into the theater, but they started locking the doors. Hundreds of black people, just running into the white neighborhoods, trashing. They started on Kensington Avenue and dumped trash all down the avenue. They came into Fishtown. There were hundreds of people fighting. The police just couldn't do nothing.

There was talk about Martin Luther King coming to Kensington. The NAACP had supported this black family. They tried to bust black people into a white community. People were afraid the neighborhood would go down if there were black people in it. There's reasons for that happening. But most people don't see those reasons. They just fear and hate.

The KKK had a car with sound equipment. They were talking about how inferior black people were. That's when the KKK and the Nazi party really came out of the closet. They stood right on the corner: guys dressed up in Nazi uniforms. There were stickers in the bathrooms of movie houses that read "Kill all niggers," with phone numbers to call. I can tell you where one is right now. I called this number and listened to their tapes a couple of times—about the size of our brains versus the size of black people's brains.

I used to live in Kensington after going through changes and try to talk to people about ways, about changes. It was really strange. Even today when I go down there, they feel uncomfortable. They don't want to say "nigger" around me. Of course, some people do it. They go out of their way to say this. I don't understand it, the ethnic thing. Even when our neighborhood was all white, people would lash out against different ethnic backgrounds. I mean, why'd they call me "Dago," looking down on me just because I was Italian? I don't understand.

Tony had learned his neighborhood's other face—its ability to hate even as it embraces its own kind, the lines it draws and the enemies it names, and the enemies it doesn't name. Why race hate?

In the Land of Opportunity "anybody," they say, "can become somebody." So if you're not much of a somebody, maybe you're a "nobody," with nobody but yourself to blame. Still, even a nobody needs to be better than somebody. This is the class function of race. Racism in our society is not primarily economic in origin. It's not a ruling-class plot to create an underclass and thus discipline white workers' wage demands with the thought of instant replaceability from below. Race in America has to do with securing an easily identifiable "bottom people" in reference to which others, battling for dignity and mostly losing, can still prop up their bruised self-esteem. "Well, at least we're better than *them!*"

Why this need for a "bottom people"—this need to know that you're not them and they're not you? The tragic irony is that if one believes the American dream, that "in America anybody is free to become somebody," then the one thing you're not free to do is *not* to become somebody—at least not without a good deal of self-blame. This is the dark side of the dream. It narrows our sense of comradeship. It turns us into lonely individuals or groups of individuals, trying to become somebody, running alongside others who are also trying to become somebody, each eyeing the other to see who's getting ahead. The result is that we cannot perceive common interests where we are. Instead, we dream of moving up. In the stampede to get ahead, we become a collection of individuals dreaming the same dream—a dream that divides us in reality even as it unites us in fantasy.

And so a silence descends upon our vastly unequal land. As middle class and working class and poor, as black and white and Hispanic, as male and female—we share a common suffering but the suffering remains mute. We cannot bear to give up that one thing we must give up if we are to gain clarity about our lives: the illusion of a society without class except a vast and mobile middle class, the illusion of opportunity for all. We think we need these illusions. We cling to them. They keep us hoping because we don't know what else to hope for. So again and again we wrap ourselves in a politics of nostalgia and embrace those who pick our pockets.

Tony Longo speaks from below. As Latin American liberation theologians would say, he "names his own reality."[4]

I was unemployed for over a year. I just couldn't find a job. It really changed me. I wasn't ready for anything like that. The realization of not finding work hit me. I went around looking. I thought, Ninety-two bucks a week from unemployment, and I can get a little job and make a few bucks, which wouldn't be hard to take. But there was nothing, not even a dishwasher job. Places with dishwasher jobs, there'd be five or six guys there who'd been washing dishes for years. I didn't stand a chance.

I went out to Sun Ship one day. They were advertising they wanted welders. I went out there and the line is all the way out the office door. There were about sixty standing there drinking coffee. A black guy tried to bust his way into the middle of the line. A big fight broke out. That was everything the science-fiction writers have been telling us about. I didn't want to get involved in the fight. I went back later, and this white guy and I was competing for the same job. This guy was working twelve years as a steel welder—there was just no hope!

I went to the unemployment office, and all they had were apple orchard pickers. They asked me to take a trainee job and pay me about $2.35 an hour. See, they wanted the labor, they just didn't want to pay. And they've done this before to working people. Before the unions, they done this.

Today the unions are corrupt. The government is even more corrupt. They are going to try to break ths unions and make us work for less money. They tried to do that to me. I seen it right there in the shipyard. Seeing that ship, and seeing the unemployment office for the first time, are probably two of the most horrifying things I seen in my life. When I say horrifying, I mean not like scary, but just seeing people being agonized, like a pain that wasn't physical. You're in the line for three and a half hours. You talk about money, earning money.

Some people, they're making it. They got this little job, and they are getting checks, and they're making it. I say that's cool. They are trying to better themselves by this. The other people that can't get work, and unemployment is too low, they have to wait there all day. And they're in physical pain because they are there physically. But mentally, they are in even worse pain because unemployment is unfair. Because once you go off unemployment you go to the welfare office—and nobody, nobody, nobody wants to be on welfare! I don't care what anybody says.

I was on welfare, off and on, since I got out of high school. But nobody *wants* to be on welfare. I seen grown men that been working at the same job fifteen years cry in the unemployment office. Because they are afraid of losing their house, or their marriage is breaking up. They're losing their cars. Everything the workers in this country wanted is going down the drain.

Longo's analysis of the complex institutional system which maintains class barriers is devastating. It shows how one-sided and distorting is the view from above that focuses upon ideas of a middle-class society with open opportunity for all. Yet the irony is that Tony ends up taking his personal hopes back to the established system and its institutions that officially certify competence. As just one person, what else can he do? Where else can he take his dreams?

I've got to have my education together before I'd want to raise a child. Because my child is going to be smart. He's not going to go to public schools. They ain't going to mess with my kids. My kids are going to be educated. They're going to be reading and writing at a very early age. It's the same thing your parents said to you: "I want to give you everything I never had." That's the same thing I want. If I'm not making good money, I'm not going to have any children. I don't want to raise them in nothing like this apartment house. I want to have my own house.

I remember being hungry when I was a kid, putting cardboard in my shoes. And people laughing at me. Always wearing the same clothes, people would always be laughing! That ain't going to happen to my kids.

The view from below can cut through the mystifying illusions of the American dream. But who wants to give up that dream? The view of America from an unemployment line can be very revealing. But who wants to stand in that line? Tony Longo still has a dream. Ironically, it takes him back to where he first was defeated—to school. A class-based system of denied opportunity becomes internalized and mystified into self-accusation.

In the end, Tony thinks his problem is that he's dumb. He experiences himself as fundamentally lacking capacity to interact with others in a way that displays capacity and effectiveness. It is not simply that he knows what it means to be unemployed. Rather, at a deeper level Tony thinks he's unemployable, incapable of managing social cooperation with others in a way that is mutually productive. His early experience in society has undermined his sense of being skilled and needed. This is the price often paid by those stuck at the bottom of our society.

Stanley Robinson was born black and poor. He made his way up to become a successful owner of two clothing stores in West Philadelphia. But he was not content with material success. For years he's been giving as much time to society as to his business. He tries, with considerable success, to place poor black men and women in private-sector jobs—jobs that he believes have a future.

He doesn't like Tony Longo's story. He thinks it invites self-pity. "Every guy I see sittin' on the street corner in the ghetto can give you this 'America isn't fair' routine. Do you know where it gets them? Right into the bar! They use it as an excuse."

Stan Robinson speaks for many who try to help—and do help!—individual unemployed and underemployed Americans break free of despair. It is the double bind of well-meaning teachers and preachers and social workers everywhere. Yes, there are structures of oppression in our society. But to encourage the disadvantaged, and therefore the already self-doubting, to focus upon these structures can lead more readily to fatalism and defeat than to organizing for social change. So we help those we can to get in and get up in the system as it is . . . and live with an uneasy conscience about the masses whom we never reach and, given the system, can never reach.

Dorothy Mims was born as poor as Tony Longo, and black and female as well. She was born in Philadelphia's worst ghetto. But she was determined not to stay there. It is her determination to better herself and her ability to apply herself to the intricacies of social escape that make her story a suitable counterpart to Longo's. Tony said, "I seen more than I was supposed to see." And, like gazing upon Medusa, it froze him in his place. Dorothy sees less widely but, perhaps because of that, she sees the way immediately before her more clearly.

We asked Dorothy what happens when she goes out of her door in the morning onto a street of broken houses, broken dreams, and broken people.[5]

It all comes down on you. It really comes down on you. In fact it's like living in two worlds. I know I want to make it. Well, first of all I know I am somebody. I would just like to be known. Because when I walk out of my house, like everyone's looking out of their window, sitting on the steps, watching every move I make. They realize that myself, as well as my sisters, and this one brother that lives across the street, are really the only people that seem to want to get ahead. Not that we're the only young people on the block. But everyone else is so preoccupied with despair. It's almost as though they've been knocked down so many times by this world that they really don't have any ambition, no pick up and go.

My parents always told me that you must have an education, that you must know people that don't want to pull you down, people that want to see you get ahead.

For Dorothy, her neighborhood was a trap, a disease called despair. She knew what happens to people when they give up, how it makes them feel guilty. She knew why others in her neighborhood wanted to pull her down in the self-excusing, self-defeating comfort of inevitability—the unspoken "our kind can't get out." But the demands of an insistent mother, who, with thirteen children to raise, ran a very tight ship at home, opened the door for Dorothy.

I had to be in bed by eight thirty on school nights. On the weekends it wasn't too much later. In the morning, we always left the house after having breakfast. No one left the house without having breakfast. Some of my friends would come to school eating potato chips, candy, that type of thing. Some of them really didn't know where their parents were that morning.

A lot of friends I would bring over to my house my mother would say, "I don't want you hanging around that girl anymore," and "I don't want you around that boy!" I never understood why.

I tried to kill myself at the age of fourteen. I can remember trying to take my life because I was so angry with my mother. She wouldn't let me be a part of what I really felt I had to be a part of. Which was to be with my friends and do the things they were doing. If you want to hang with these people you can't be different from them.

Today, when I see these people, they're hooked on drugs—not saying they were destined to do that, but it was something my mother could see. I live in a neighborhood where all my old friends are, and I'm about the only one attending college from that crowd I used to be with.

Some of them, I don't know, it seems like they're ashamed of themselves. They don't really want me to see them. They duck in their house real fast. Most of the women have a lot of kids. None of them are older than twenty-three. I see a lot of my old girlfriends that have two, three children now. Some of them are pregnant again. I think they're trapped for life.

So I am happy that my mother told me, "No, that's not the way for you to go. You go this way." She was constantly pushing me. "You have to have this. You have to have that." And I really appreciate that. I think without that I couldn't have made it.

It wasn't school that helped Dorothy escape. School, she said, "hadn't taught me anything." Rather, it was middle-class family values—values of neatness and punctuality, of dependable home routine, of sorting your friends and wanting to get ahead. Once out of the ghetto she would have to contend with being black in a society where whites are predominant and dominant. But already she knew that to let that get to you is a dead-end road. Of her friends she said, "I think they're trapped for life."

You have to sort your friends. Not everyone wants to get where you want to go. And when I moved from home, I found that I had really learned something, something that I needed. If my parents hadn't instilled that certain thing in me—you know, "Get ahead; do this and do that"—then I'd probably be like a lot of these children I see today, walking the streets and feeling nothing and doing nothing.

In 1971 when I left North Philadelphia, the ghetto, and went to Hartford, Connecticut, the suburb, I really realized that I was black and poor. I felt ignorant, especially in college. There were so many kids that were really advanced, not only in accounting but just the simple things that I should have known long ago. I remember once I got to the Hartford Institute of Accounting, I wrote the principal of Simon Gratz [High School] a letter. I told him that they hadn't taught me anything in school. I felt like I had graduated from an elementary school. Simple things, such as English and mathematics, that I should have known from junior high school, I didn't know. I had to learn all that, plus the college level. And I felt very slow; I felt left out.

That was the first time I had felt my color, and felt that it was against me rather than for me.

We asked Dorothy, "How do you make it? How do you do that as a black woman in a society dominated by white money?" She snapped back:

And white *males* at that! How do you do that? [laughing, eyes dancing] You wear a lot of miniskirts! No, I'm only joking. How do you do that?

I shouldn't say this, but part of the reason I got over, so to speak, in college was mostly a matter of self-respect. That got me across. It really did. Conversing with people, they really thought I was smart. I knew that I didn't really know that much. But I knew enough to keep my mouth shut and show nothing but my manners and my self-respect, until I got to know lots of things that they already knew.

"My manners and my self-respect" got Dorothy Mims off West Diamond Street in Philadelphia. She left behind her neighborhood, her friends, and her family (who didn't in fact make it out of the ghetto). "I was always a loner," Dorothy said. It was the price she paid to get out.

Dorothy looked at the world more narrowly than Tony did. She looked at her neighborhood where her friends were getting stuck, and she wanted out. She had parents who were ambitious for her, parents who pushed her on. Things were a little less destroyed in Tony's neighborhood. The need to escape was not so obvious. In Kensington a working-class value system was still in place where respect did not depend upon success at competitive individualism but upon loyalty to family and hard work (even if not well-paid). In Kensington there were values that helped shelter working-class dignity, if one accepted one's class status.

But Tony looked at the picture of America more comprehensively, and it left him feeling powerless and trapped. His family and his friends didn't see what he saw. Instead of creating a community of speech, what he saw (that others didn't) drove him into silence. Perhaps if he had not seen as clearly, he would have felt more at home in Kensington and taken the cops' advice—to buy sneakers and wear khakis and be a regular guy. Only he couldn't have taken his father's job. The city of Philadelphia lost almost half its industrial jobs in the decade between 1970 and 1980. One of those jobs belonged to Tony's father.

Radicals probably find Tony's view from below the important one. But service workers on the front line in the ghetto probably find Dorothy's hope more immediate and practical. In fact neither Tony's nor Dorothy's view from below contradict the other. Those who want to force a choice between the two don't understand. Before there can be clarity, there must be hope. And hope is more like a habit than a sudden discovery. It is a degree of energy and focus in one's life before it is a plan for one's future.

Dorothy's middle-class values—her household routines, her mother insisting she "sort her friends," her growing conviction of her own self-worth—these must be seen not as cutting a different direction from critical awareness and social activism but as qualities of everyday life that many of us are lucky enough to take for granted and are the cultural foundations upon which a more radical perspective can be built. Profound disorganization of everyday life is not fertile ground for critical social analysis or for political organizing. Dorothy's having "my manners and my self-respect" defends her basic sense of capacity. She is less profoundly injured than Tony.

What Tony has that the rest of us need is a firm fix on the reality and meaning of class in our society: how institutions of authority, perhaps quite unintentionally but nevertheless effectively, operate to maintain this system of class and how, until that fact is addressed, Dorothy will be among the lucky few who escape. What Dorothy can teach Tony is that persons have to get on with their lives in spite of that fact—because blaming the odds against your making it on the system too often turns out to be a way of denying responsibility for your life and giving up.

What Tony needs is a community of shared speaking and listening, like the base communities of the churches in Latin America. In Latin America, the church of the people has discovered that it is crucial to join the people *where they are*—especially if where they are is deeply enmeshed in despair—and encourage them to name their reality. No one else can do our naming for us. In speaking and in being heard and responded to, we gain confidence, broaden our perspective, and begin to believe in our right to protest. The listeners support those who have just found voice in their task of liberating themselves from silence, from humiliation, from dependency and feelings of being incapable of self-direction. That is what the biblical command "Love thy neighbor" means. Real charity is finding out how much the rest of us can learn from the poor and then letting them teach us.[6]

Unfortunately, Tony remains alone and silent. You and I may hear his words and perhaps partly believe them. But he himself does not believe them: Tony illustrates the tragedy of people who lose heart. "I'm dumb; just really incomplete." They do not complain, they drink too much. They do not protest, they take dope. They blame themselves. Or they blame the system but do not fight back, and they embrace their injuries and refuse to feel responsible for what's happening to their lives.

Dorothy is alone too. More alone than she yet knows. Hers is the aloneness of that vast togetherness called "I just want to become somebody." She escaped the ghetto, but at the price of leaving family and friends behind. She has gotten into the race to get ahead, running alongside others who are also trying to get ahead. But it is a race that has no end or sense of sure foundation.

We have been listening to the voices of the unemployed and the underemployed, the voices of the new poor and the voices of the old poor who have been stuck at the bottom of our society for generations. These realities in our society—the injuries and insults that happen to a Mary Duranko and a Tony Longo or the neighborhood of despair as described by Dorothy Mims—these did not develop out of a vacuum. They emerged out of contradictions in our culture's values which have shaped our way of dwelling together. Central in this value heritage is our society's view of work. We will examine this view of work in the next two chapters. It is the necessary next step if we are to pass beyond sympathetic listening and begin to think about changes in public policy.

6

Work and Democracy

Dorothy and Tony wanted to show the world they were some-body. They wanted to prove themselves through their work, even if that meant nothing more than attaining steady employment. Proof of self-worth through success in work is part of the American dream, whether we are working on that dream at the bottom of our society or at the top. What we often do not notice is that this value we attach to work—that we seek by way of our work to prove our-selves worthy—stands in fundamental contradiction to the demo-cratic values that are also a part of our heritage. Because democracy, the right of all to participate in governing society, depends upon people who do not believe their worth is something they need to prove. It depends upon the presumption that each person has worth and deserves a say in society simply because of being a member of that society.

Perhaps the main reason we seldom insist upon democratic con-trol in the economic realm is that at work we are trying to prove ourselves worthy of respect, and therefore we remain unsure about how much we have a right to demand. We make an artificial division in our lives. At work we think of ourselves as individuals hoping for success; we confine our sense of democratic rights—our right to have a say in control—to electoral politics. It is our view of work that is the fundamental issue here: whether we see work as the arena of acquiring private possessions and proving self-worth or as the ex-pression of social cooperation and the context of democratic con-trol.

"I did it for myself and so should you" is a widespread sentiment reflective of how we see our relationship to others in society. "I worked for it, I earned it, and it's mine!" is a remarkably popular expression and, standing by itself, also remarkably inaccurate. It displays little awareness of how our personal well-being is inextrica-

bly intertwined with that of others, how what individually we earn
has mostly been earned for us by generations of workers who cultivated this earth before us and who left us their skills. Still, not
needing others as the definition of strength represents a perspective
upon self and society that is deeply rooted in our culture. "Freedom" for many of those fleeing the Old World to the New meant
freedom *from* constraint, freedom *from* others, freedom in the land
of freedom to be your own person.

But autonomy is only one part of freedom, perhaps its lesser part.
For example, if you are one of five survivors of a plane crash trapped
deep in the Alaskan forest, and none of you speak the same language, clearly freedom is discovering a way of cooperating. This,
too, was a value learned by the early immigrants to this country. The
new land was harsh and survival precarious. Sustenance and shelter
were common tasks—sometimes a shared success and at other times
a common and calamitous failure. This freedom through our work
with others to get things done that one cannot do alone is at least
as fundamental in our common memory as freedom *from* others to
do what individually we want.

Our value heritage is divided and contradictory concerning the
meaning of work. If we are going to think clearly about how to
achieve *better* work, we will have to take up a position on this dis-
agreement. Take, for example, the notion that by my work I make
things "my own."

"In the beginning all the world was America," complained John
Locke in his *Second Treatise of Government,* a writing published in 1690
that was to influence profoundly the framers of our Constitution.[1]
What was it about America that so irritated Locke? In 1690 he saw
mostly the land of native Americans: land not fenced in, land not
privately acquired, land therefore not systematically cultivated—in
short, land not yet harnessed to human ambition. He went on:
"Where there is not something, both lasting and scarce, and so
valuable to be hoarded up, there men [sic] will not be apt to enlarge
their possessions of land."[2] Only where there is a money economy
does it make sense to begin to dream of *more,* to want *more,* to plant
and reap *more.* With money comes limitless horizons of economic
expansion and so, crucially, an imagination fired with ambition.

The news announced by Locke, news that was to bring forth a new
political and economic order in the West, was that people don't
need to be poor. People can want—should want—*more.* Harness this
"wanting" to the right of private ownership of the fruits of one's
labor, and the result will literally be a new world—a world of rapidly
expanding material well-being never before dreamed of, much less

enjoyed. You can see why such ideas would influence deeply the founders of our own nation, many of whom shared Locke's ambition for a different America, one whose land was privately owned—*by the white folks.* Freedom for Locke is freedom *from* the encroachment of others to enjoy what we have privately acquired. It is each person's freedom, as he puts it, "to order their actions, and dispose of their possessions and persons, as they see fit . . . without asking leave, or depending upon the will of any other."[3]

This view of the relationship between work and freedom was to cross the Atlantic and find powerful advocates on our own shores. Hard work and self-reliance became for us powerful cultural ideals. Ralph Waldo Emerson spoke of this. Manliness, he argued, is the inner strength to stand alone and provide for oneself. "Welcome evermore to gods and men is the *self-helping* man. For him all doors are flung wide; him all tongues greet, all honors crown, all eyes follow with desire."[4]

Emerson found his true vocation, after a false start in the Unitarian ministry—a calling he renounced in 1832—as a star lecturer on the lyceum circuit. His immense popularity, beginning in the Boston area but then spreading throughout the country, indicated that he stated publicly the private thoughts and values of many of his fellow Americans. Work, for Emerson, does not connect us but instead allows us to stand apart from others. "It is only as a man puts off all foreign support and stands alone that I see him to be strong and to prevail."[5]

Emerson was familiar with Darwin. But unlike the biologist, who found no rational purpose steering nature's evolution, Emerson saw the Mind of God at work there.

> Nature is the symbol of spirit. The use of natural history is to give us aid in supernatural history. . . . Man is conscious of a universal soul within or behind his individual life, wherein, as in a firmament, the natures of Justice, Truth, Love, Freedom, arise and shine. This universal soul, he calls Reason: it is not mine, or thine, or his, but we are its; we are its property and men.[6]

This mystical individualism (in the mid-nineteenth century called Transcendentalism) legitimated a most singular sense of unconnectedness to others. The self, in its own self-understanding, simply bypasses social relationships and goes without pause to the Universal Soul. "I have taught one doctrine," Emerson wrote in his journals, "the infinitude of the private man."[7]

Said directly, there is simply no principle of gratitude in any of this. For Emerson, the self belongs only to itself or, more accurately, in its aloneness only to God. Self-reliance is God-reliance, and any other human reliances invade and dilute the purity of this liberty which sets me free boldly to be myself.

This confidence in one's inner light should lead to a profound sense of calm. But it needs defending.

> At times the whole world seems to be in conspiracy to importune you with emphatic trifles. Friend, client, child, sickness, fear, want, charity, all knock at once at thy closet door and say—"Come out unto us." But keep thy state; come not into their confusion. The power men possess to annoy me I give them by a weak curiosity.[8]

Others might want to call this "curiosity" sympathy, a sense of shared exposure, a knowledge of common suffering. But not Emerson! "Do not tell me, as a good man did to-day, of my obligation to put all poor men in good situations. Are they *my* poor? I tell thee, thou foolish philanthropist, that I grudge the dollar, the dime, the cent I give to such men as do not belong to me and to whom I do not belong."[9]

This understanding of the relationship of self to others in society stands as a classic statement of that part of our cultural heritage which sees the American hero symbolized in the self-reliant man, whose work frees him from needing or depending upon others. For Emerson, and for that significant part of the American value heritage he speaks for, work is *my* work, what I do and earn for myself. It is not *our* work or our collaboration in society (which would pose the issue of democratic control).

It is important to note in this regard that Emerson's view of work is profoundly gender-biased, as is his view of human strength. Neither his definition of work nor his definition of human virtue shows any knowledge at all of women's traditional work and strength in the nurturing of human relatedness. Emerson's "manliness" is just that —what he thinks a *male* can and should be. Moreover, Emerson's God is equally gender-biased—no passionate or suffering God, but an aloof God of cold Eternities, a God who teaches us neither repentence nor justice but a calm and well-defended self-possession.[10]

But from the beginning there was also another God in America, and with that different God a different picture of the American Way. The Puritan and Pilgrim experiments planted on our soil the notion of a common good—a "Commonwealth"—more fundamental, more real, more morally compelling than any collection of individual success stories. More than three hundred years ago John Winthrop, first governor of the colony that was soon to be established at Massachusetts Bay, spoke to his followers on the deck of the ship that was taking them to their new world.

> Now the only way to avoid shipwreck and to provide for our posterity is to follow the counsel of Micah: to do justly, to love mercy, to walk humbly with our God. For this end, we must be knit together in this work as one man [sic]. We must entertain each other in brotherly affection; we must be willing to abridge ourselves of our superfluities, for the supply of others' necessities; we must uphold a familiar commerce together. We must delight in each other, make others' conditions our own, rejoice together, mourn together, labor and suffer together.

But then Winthrop warned, echoing the words of Deuteronomy:

> There is now set before us life and good, death and evil, in that we are commanded this day to love the Lord our God, to walk in His ways and to keep His laws and the articles of our covenant with Him, that we may live and be multiplied, and that the Lord our God may bless us in the land whither we go to possess it; but if our hearts shall turn away so that we will not obey, but shall be seduced and worship . . . other gods, our pleasures and profits, and serve them, it is propounded unto us this day, we shall surely perish out of the good land whither we pass over this vast sea to possess it.[11]

A God who in the broad reaches of history seeks neither self-reliance nor individual success but requires *social justice*—a reckoning no nation can escape—speaks for a different American Way from the one we hear and see most often today. Today, the vision of the good society which receives unquestioning admiration from many is a society of free, industrious, and prosperous *individuals*, who leave each other alone except where self-interest persuades them to join together.

Unwittingly, such individualistic values which many people attach to work move against the democratic values to which we also claim loyalty. Sometimes this is easier to see from the margins of society. Tony Longo saw the paradox of power in our society—how we proclaim ourselves a democracy while leaving power, especially economic power, in the hands of the few. But Longo did not connect this insight to his personal hopes to prove his worth through success. In the end, Tony's view of freedom remained contradictory.

That was not the case with Martin Luther King, Jr. His life story reveals a remarkable pilgrimage in coming to terms with the central contradictions of our culture's values. King began his public career in Montgomery, Alabama, in 1955 protesting the denial of individual rights to black Americans—rights to sit down on a bus or be served at a lunch counter. His career ended thirteen years later, in 1968, in Memphis, Tennessee, where he had gone to join the trash collectors of that city, who were on strike for higher wages. From individual freedoms to the collective realitites of class and power and who controls the economy—this slow but steady transformation marked the pilgrimage Martin Luther King, Jr., took in the task of searching out the realities of our society.

What was it that King sought? "Freedom," he said again and again. Was this freedom for blacks individually to "become somebody"? That is what many thought. But in fact King had a much deeper grasp of our society's fundamental paradox. The freedom King sought was the freedom of blacks to be recognized for what they already were—*part of America*—and the right to be included and listened to as equal citizens. In his letter from Birmingham jail, he said:

> We will reach the goal of freedom in Birmingham, and all over the nation, because the goal of America is freedom. Abused and scorned though we may be, our destiny is tied up with America's destiny. Before the pilgrim landed at Plymouth, we were here. Before the pen of Jefferson etched the majestic words of the Declaration of Independence across the pages of history, we were here. For more than two centuries our forebears labored in this country without wages. . . . If the inexpressible cruelties of slavery could not stop us, the oppression we now face will surely fail. We will win our freedom because the sacred heritage of our nation and the eternal will of God are embodied in our echoing demands.[12]

The values of inclusion and participation which inspired King were ideals he had learned from biblical religion as preached in black churches, where the story of Moses and Pharaoh and the freedom of a whole people from economic and political bondage (not just the individualistic escape of Moses to Midian) took on meanings that were never simply abstract or otherworldly.

King put into words and actions a freedom that was far more than my freedom to get ahead of you, of my group to get ahead of your group. His politics remained far from the politics of "if I win, you lose; and if you win, I lose." Against those who encourage ideas of winning by defeating, of speaking by silencing others who want to speak, King argued powerfully for that part of the American value heritage which seeks democracy—the recognition by each of the other's inalienable dignity, of the equal right of each to be heard, and of how out of this speaking and listening all realize a good that none can grasp alone. It was a search for freedom that led him from the civil rights movement of Montgomery to the economic issue of power posed at Memphis.

Preoccupation with personally making it undermines the politics of democracy. We do not reach out to those around us—who share our own realities—because we are so busy reaching out to those above us. That is why the recovery of democratic rule depends upon a firm grasp on our society's class realitites. "Middle-class society" and "opportunity for all" are myths, not realities—myths that we may love and need because they keep us hoping, but also myths that legitimate privilege and deflect anger at social injury back upon the self, or upon those behind us in the race to get ahead. If we really think "our betters" *are* our betters, we will never join together with our own kind—the vast majority—in order to rule.

These contradictory meanings we assign to work will be played out inside our common life in either of two very different scenarios. Times of slow economic growth, such as we now face, may reawaken our sense of community and our desire for shared control. Like a family getting over a spending binge where no one needed to set priorities and everyone just took more and more, perhaps harder times will restart a public discussion over priorities. Unfortunately, the price we paid in recent decades for consuming ever more has been less and less real participation, fewer and fewer experiences of sharing our skills as workers and as citizens. In our affluence we became more isolated, mistakenly convinced that we did not need others. But harder times may bring people who used to think they didn't need each other back together.

We can have a fair America that is also an abundant America—only not lavishly abundant for the few. We can have a land where average folks have an effective say—only we must believe that what they have to say is something we need to hear.

Or perhaps we will act out of the other side of the paradox, which would lead us during times of slow economic growth to scapegoat more furiously and demand control (deflected and misdirected) over those who are already relatively powerless.

In his *The Crucible of Race,* author Joel Williamson studied the rise of radical racism in the South, beginning about 1889, which witnessed a dramatic upsurge of lynchings, many of them before huge crowds. A string of race riots was fomented in which mobs of whites would invade black neighborhoods, attacking the occupants. As the reason for all this, Williamson points out that the turn of the century saw a massive displacement of farm workers, as the Industrial Revolution was eventually to reduce the number of farm workers in our society from 38 percent in 1900 to 3.8 percent today. The race radicals in the South experienced a crisis of power. Unable to control their life situations either economically or politically, they looked elsewhere.

> The result was that Southern white men were unable to play their role of protector-as-breadwinner with the satisfaction to which they always aspired and had sometimes achieved. Embattled, white men picked up and emphasized another part of the role, the protector-as-defender of the purity of their women, in this instance against the imagined threat from the black beast rapist. Lynching and rioting, total disfranchisement, and blatant segregation formed satisfying displays of power in one area of their lives when they could no longer display power in another.[13]

What Williamson does not perceive is that the attitude displayed toward women by the race radicals was just as pervaded by the compulsive need for control as was their attitude toward blacks. The woman is pictured as defenseless before the "black beast." Her sexuality is to remind her of how she cannot depend upon herself —how much she needs the white male to protect her. Having lost control over their work, white males demanded control over women and blacks. Misplaced anger redirected their energy from the world of real power to a world of illusory compensations.

Today, we are undergoing what many economists refer to as "the second Industrial Revolution," with millions of workers (mostly male) in manufacturing and heavy industry experiencing loss of economic control. Whether harder times will take us toward a renewal of democracy or toward a displaced need to demean and control groups in our society already lacking power is not yet clear.

Our culture's heritage makes contradictory assessments concerning the meaning of work and the relationship of the self to others in society. If we are going to come to sound conclusions on the future of work in America, we must take up a position within this divided heritage. For our part, we have tried to make clear that human work is not first of all a means of making things our own but a way of collaborating with others. Human work is both *skilled* work and *shared* work. It is social and historical.

If we are to bring democratic rule to bear upon the way we organize our economy, then we must see the simple truth that work is not primarily what we do to make a living or to prove our personal worth. Work *is* human living, a direct expression of a unique human dignity. Therefore work *as such,* not its product (wealth or validation of worth), deserves our direct and serious attention. How we work together largely determines how we live together. Because of this, democracy must also become economic democracy or it will not long remain democracy at all.

In our own time, we are faced with a new global economy which requires us to rethink our understanding and organization of the way we work, especially of who owns and controls the economy. In the final chapters of this book, we will clarify what it means to view and interpret work in terms of social solidarity rather than individual success. We begin with the bewildering variety of personal "work ethics" which are presently expressed by different groups in our society. Can the religious idea of *vocation* bring clarity to the discussion of work or only further the confusion?

7

Vocation and Community

After her husband received the news that his already pared-down job was going to be eliminated, Linda Gilroy wrote:

> Why is God letting this happen to all of us? It begins to rock your foundation. And in some deep part of me, I know that that is what it is meant to do. It is being done for some purpose, and I wish I didn't realize that.

For many of us, how we think about work—individually and as a society—is so woven into our ways of being that it remains unconscious, invisible, unspoken. That is, until something goes wrong. Linda and Pat did not often talk about their philosophy of work, that which brought meaning to their labor and got them out of bed on Monday morning. They both had a belief, however, deeply engrained and rarely articulated, that not only did their work help them to survive and support their child but that in some way it was related to a larger purpose. To be sure, for Linda and Pat work is identified with a paycheck, as it is for millions of North Americans. But after Pat was laid off, not only was the paycheck gone, they also felt left out of participation in the Grand Scheme, even at cross purposes with it. God was punishing them or teaching them something through their misery, they felt. The work ethic that had once provided cohesion to their life now caused confusion. Like a boomerang, it had turned on them to complicate their suffering.

Discussion of a "work ethic" is often thought to be only the concern of eighteenth-century Puritans, nineteenth-century philosophers, or twentieth-century unionists. This especially seems to be the case today. These are the days of pragmatism, not reflection. Presently the priority is simply to have a job and keep it, rather than to contemplate questions of its meaning. "Why should I worry about having a 'theology of work' when I just need to find a job?"

Part of the disillusionment, as we have seen, stems from the dawning realization that having a clearly understood work ethic hasn't really gotten us very far as a society. For many, like Pat and Linda, it has actually backfired. They struggle to find an ethic that will provide meaning and motivation in a changing work world.

Before a reformulation can occur, however, we must first understand the particular conceptions of work that already operate in our culture. And there are many. We used to speak of the Protestant work ethic as the universally held and understood doctrine to which our country and its citizens ascribe: a doctrine of individual labor that results in self-sufficiency and self-betterment. Historically, it is the public philosophy which spawned the American dream. The phrase Protestant work ethic has become so entrenched in our culture that it has become an assumption of our national consciousness. However, the concept has become nebulous and, in light of the economic crisis, increasingly unable to confer meaning on our work. One has only to listen to the language of the workplace to understand that a variety of different understandings of work actually exist in our society. The Protestant work ethic has been broken down and reshaped by the economic realities we experience.

The various ways in which we now think about work—our philosophy, theology, or ethic of work—inform our actions and choices, both individually and collectively. They operate as the often unarticulated determinates guiding the decisions of corporations, unions, government agencies, and individual workers. They inform our perceptions of ourselves and each other. They define who is successful, what a "wise" business decision is, and who it is that we respect (or look down upon). Our work ethic helps society to structure and interpret power relationships, whether between wife and husband, boss and laborer, or even first and third world. It is, in other words, an active and integral part of our life together.

But there is no longer one uniform work ethic bringing the comfort of a shared understanding to our society. In fact, the disparities among workers are widening. How we approach and experience our work is becoming more and more diversified as the quality and the availability of work change. For some in our society, work is seen as a duty or calling, for others a punishment, and for still others a commodity to be bought and sold. For some, work is creative, but for a growing number of others it is stultifying. For some it is indistinguishable from leisure activity, but for many more it *buys* leisure. As the major investment of human energy, it is both craved and cursed. Individual identification with one's work covers a spectrum from deep alienation to complete identification. One worker says, "I *am* my work. Retirement would be like death for me. I can't imagine life without my work." In the next office another worker is counting minutes until coffee break, days until Friday, or how many "mental health days" are left this year.

Work Ethics in Today's Culture

If there are different work ethics operating in our culture, how can they best be identified? Perhaps the best indicator of the meaning attached to work is the expression of motivation. Meaning and motivation are intimately related. "I work because . . ." belies the deeper understanding one has of the meaning of one's work. Again, our motivations run the gamut. We work because we "have to," "love to," "need to, for money," "want to, for status," or "are called to." We work for ourselves or for others—families, constituents, society. Obviously, those who work because they have to, and whose job experience gives them little opportunity for satisfaction, will have a very different perspective on the meaning of work from those who can say they sometimes enjoy their work so much they get lost in it and look forward to Monday morning as well as to Friday afternoon.

Of course, there have always been differences in the ways people have experienced their work. There have been, and will always be, some jobs that are pure drudgery and others that are more rewarding. However, in 1984 for the first time there were more people serving hamburgers at McDonald's than there were producing steel for the nation's largest steel manufacturer, U.S. Steel. And for $7 to $10 an hour less! Not only does this reflect the dramatic trends of job creation in this country, it foreshadows predictable shifts in our work philosophies.

Before we can speculate what a future work ethic might look like, we must turn first to the historical and cultural development of the attitudes toward work expressed today. These did not, after all, take root spontaneously or in isolation. The heritage of our various work ethics has operated historically on the factory line and in the boardroom—interpreting not only how we experience work but how it is structured and shaped.

Work as Achievement

It is appropriate to begin with the early Puritans—those credited with most consistently articulating and embodying the Protestant work ethic. In the second and third generations of these Protestant immigrants, what began as a communal ideal (the commonwealth of Governor John Winthrop) degenerated slowly into an individualized work ethic.

For these doctrinaire believers, work had to do with one's salvation. Although one could not earn salvation (this was unilaterally up to Divine discretion), industrious labor and material wealth were signs of one's election. The harder one worked, and the more prosperous one became, the more certain one could be about personal salvation.[1] This bred a motivation for individual achievement, a moral intolerance for laziness, a certain self-righteousness, and an often insufferable ambition. The Puritan legacy is manifested today in compulsive workaholism even when it leads to the self-defeating point of burnout.

The symbols of salvation have undergone change in the evolution of our culture. Professionals today are as eager as any of their Puritan forebears to demonstrate their status and righteousness. But the "election" they seek is more squarely in this world than the next. For those whose work becomes part of a career-building strategy, the trek remains as individualistic as it became for the Puritans. A preoccupation with personal status continues to be the central motivator, although the sought-after goal is more likely materialistic than metaphysical. From Cotton Mather to Horatio Alger to the One Minute Manager, the strain of public philosophy known as the Protestant work ethic has provided a piety and cultural context in which work has become the means to a personalistic goal. On the path to "getting ahead," workers have become isolated from one another and from public commitment. After all, to demonstrate salvation or professional competence, one must distinguish oneself from all others. Through work, the burden of proof is on workers to show that they are apart from and above the *hoi polloi*. The accent here is on achievement, not service—unless that service contributes to one's individual achievement. But the Protestant work ethic in its present expression, far from being the public consensus, is relevant to a shrinking number of middle-class professionals.

George Gray was a Southern textile entrepreneur who subscribed to the ethic of work-as-achievement. The early Protestant work ethic was the legacy of his own philosophy, and the Industrial Revolution the context that shaped it. The words on his gravestone, composed by his pastor, indicate to his peers that his success reflected salvation in both the material and spiritual realms.

A CAPTAIN OF INDUSTRY
A PIONEER OF PROSPERITY
BY INDUSTRY AND HONESTY HE ACHIEVED SUCCESS
BY JUSTICE AND MAGNANIMITY
HE WON THE RESPECT AND LOVE OF HIS FELLOW MEN
BY FAITH IN CHRIST
HE BUILT A CHRISTIAN CHARACTER[2]

Through his work, it was thought, Mr. Gray achieved the status he had sought—in this world and the next. Service to humanity was a by-product of personal achievement, not its primary goal. Following in this tradition, a contemporary professional might also want to be remembered in the same way: the glowing sum total of a lifetime of work rewarded by wealth and social recognition.

Work as Service

Although the influence of the Protestant work ethic has been formidable, if not dominant, there have been other understandings of the meaning of work that have been transmitted through the culture. For the early Pietists—those for whom religious experience was more definitive than doctrine alone—the activity of work was in and of itself meaningful as the expression of one's faith. They too sought a certitude of blessing in their "joyful labor," but without the compelling ambition to climb to the top. The Pietists, therefore, could be found more often among the working classes than with the entrepreneurs.[3]

They drew their theological rationale from Paul's first letter to the Corinthians (chapter 7, verses 20–21, 24):

> Every one should remain in the state in which he was called. Were you a slave when called? Never mind. . . . So, brethren, in whatever state each was called, there let him remain with God.

Although Paul is referring to the call to faith in Christ, it was identified by Luther and later commentators with occupation. Ambition afforded one nothing religiously; getting ahead would not increase one's chance or certainty of salvation. In fact, it could detract from the discipline of finding satisfaction in serving God in whatever station of life one found oneself.

There are workers today who also shun ambition; "getting ahead" seems unattractive or impossible. They prefer to "just do my job," not "bothering anyone" or being bothered. Like the early

Pietists, they extract satisfaction from simply doing the work at hand. Found in all job categories, among them are those who, through varying degrees of choice, work at home. Without the social validation of promotion, status, or salary, they have had to find other sources of satisfaction and meaning.

A woman's work is never done . . . or paid for, or recognized, or honored or commended, the old feminist poster says gloomily. This certainly communicates the low level of dignity afforded the unpaid domestic labor of homemakers in our culture. Yet homemakers have developed their own work ethic in spite of society. It is an ethic born out of the need for emotional survival and self-respect.

This becomes apparent, ironically, in our interviews with men in Johnstown. One effect of unemployment for them is that it often upsets gender roles and puts them suddenly in the sphere of "women's work"—a reality that compounds their grief as they first begin spending their days at home. And yet, when faced with the dissonance between their long-held work ethic (which found meaning through their ability to support their families), and their new behavior in a domestic role, a change of heart often takes place. Without the possibility of monetary reward, social recognition, or job advancement, there is a need to find meaning and satisfaction in their new work role. The very activity of work (even housework for these men) satisfies the need for human dignity and self-respect in labor. Here is former steelworker Barry George:

I'm proud of what I do because a lot of men do not do it. Like for instance, last week I washed and took care of all the clothes. I clean, I keep the house up. As far as the kids and that, now there ain't much I don't do or don't know how to do. I do it well. I'm not a half-assed-type cleaner. You could talk to my wife or any of the neighbors.

Without romanticizing the often mundane and repetitive tasks of parenting and housework, the work ethic that has developed among domestic workers is most akin to that of the early Pietist. "Remaining in their station," women seek satisfaction in service performed for others rather than in status and prosperity earned for themselves.

That is not to say that social validation or recognition by the community is not necessary. Having one's work appreciated and validated externally as well as internally is a universal need, whatever the job description or work ethic.

Work as Curse

In the American black tradition, a work ethic emerged in which labor was seen neither as a symbol of blessedness nor opportunity for service. Work was rather seen as a vehicle of the curse and, as such, identified with suffering. This interpretation of work was drawn historically from the biblical story of an angry God's judgment on a fallen humanity:

> Cursed is the ground because of you;
>   in toil you shall eat of it all the days of your life . . .
> In the sweat of your face
>   you shall eat bread
> till you return to the ground.
>
> Genesis 3:17, 19

In terms of the white religion they had inherited, all that black people could expect from work was toil and sweat. Their work as slaves, and later as low-wage laborers, would not result in socioeconomic upward mobility but could only be endured. Herein was its meaning. Death came as a welcome release. Although their white Christian sisters and brothers gravitated to the pre-fall injunctive to "subdue the earth" when interpreting their understanding of work, work as curse was the ethic born out of slavery. It is the deepest expression of alienation from work.

Although slavery has long been outlawed in this country, the ethic of work as curse has continued—within and well beyond the black community. There are many workers today who would resonate with the old blues song:

> Well, the blues ain't nothin'
>   But a workingman feelin' bad.
> Well, it's one of the worst old feelin's
>   That any poor man's ever had.[4]

According to theologian James Cone, the blues are not a means of either adapting to or changing a situation, but of giving voice to the suffering it engenders.[5]

Work is the occasion of suffering for many workers today who thank God when it's Friday and they can have a temporary reprieve from the workaday curse. When hard work does not result in anything except poverty or close to it, it is not joyful, lucrative, or creative. It does not buy social status, nor is it the sign of eternal reward. Workers can only take satisfaction in not being dependent on the state for support—although in their discouragement it is often hard to see why that is still important. The final insult is that the worker is powerless to transform his or her own work.

Work as Commodity

With the advent of the Industrial Revolution, laborers moved from the field to the factory. A new variation on the work ethic came into being: work as commodity. Workers bought and sold their time and skills, depending on the supply available and the demand of industry for their labor. It is no wonder, then, that today work has become so identified with the price it commands that we routinely speak of what someone is "worth." A chief executive officer of a large corporation is said to be "worth" a million dollars a year, and a miner may be described as being "only worth" twenty thousand. For the most part, the price of labor is determined according to what the market will bear, as it is for any other commodity in our economy. Years of experience, personal risk, expenditure of energy, contribution to society, and preparation are not a significant part of the equation when calculating "worth."

The price tags which are put on the human activity of work are easily internalized into the individual psyche. If I am, as a typist, paid $13,000 a year, I *feel* I am worth less than my boss, who is paid $36,000. I am more expendable, a replaceable part. Leaving the company and trying to sell the commodity of my work elsewhere only confirms the low level of my worth in society.

The message of worth also becomes engrained in the collective psyche, particularly as jobs become segregated by gender and race. Women and minorities have been channeled into job categories that generally pay less than those more traditionally filled by white males. For example, recently the City of Philadelphia posted two job openings. The first was for a librarian with a master's degree in library science and required two years' experience. The salary offered was $16,000. Beside it on the bulletin board was another job, also with the city, as a "streetlight maintainance worker." There was no experience required, and only a high school diploma was necessary. The salary offered was $18,000.

Who did the city expect would fill the jobs? It was likely that a woman would be hired for the first and a man for the second. The salaries were obviously calculated not according to skill, education, or experience but according to what the market would bear. In a market in which the operating work ethic is work-as-commodity, the message becomes clear: The labor of some, in this case women, is worth less than that of others.

How does this message, when internalized, affect an individual's own work ethic? Can I still believe in myself enough to get ahead while I am also receiving the not-so-subtle message that I am not worth very much to society? The ethic of work as commodity is not just the guiding principle of multinational corporations who transfer factories to markets of cheap labor around the world. Nor is it just an economic term to help us understand how the value of work is determined in our economy. Much more than that, it is a strain of our public philosophy which interprets the meaning of human work for individuals in our society. It is quite distinct from the Protestant work ethic that evolved from the early Puritans. For all their hang-ups, they did not objectify their labor as a commodity to be bought and sold, thus allowing the marketplace to define human worth. To those who worshiped the Creator, the very thought would have been appalling, pagan, and heretical. As their legacy has eroded, we have allowed the marketplace to shape our understanding of human labor and its worth. This has been to the particular detriment to those who are less marketable in our society—women and minorities, unskilled and semiskilled workers, unemployed and underemployed workers, younger and older workers, those with handicapping physical conditions, and the growing number of non-management employees in dead-end positions that offer no chance of advancement. For this sizable chunk of the work force in our society, how they understand the meaning of work is related to how their work is valued by society. And their work is *not* valued! In response, they do not value their work and seek meaning not in their job but in their life after work hours.

Work as a Basic Human Right

Although they may have been overdrawn for the purpose of analysis, these are the theologies or philosophies of work currently coming out of the experience of North American workers. Are they the only options for a public understanding of work? Projecting any of these into the arena of our economic future is frightening. A society that makes decisions out of an understanding of work as individual careerism, or non-paid service, or a dehumanizing necessary evil, or a mere commodity is not an attractive or hopeful vision.

There is an increasing chorus of voices advocating work as a basic human right, reflective of the inherent and universal dignity of human beings. Unionists and humanists have historically been associated with this message, but they have been joined more recently by those within the religious community. The Draft of the American Catholic Bishops' Pastoral Letter on the Economy states:

> The most urgent priority for U.S. domestic economic policy is the creation of new jobs with adequate pay and decent working conditions. The prime goal must be to make it possible for *everyone who is seeking a job to find employment which befits human dignity.* [6]

They have been joined by their brothers and sisters in the Protestant community who are also speaking out on economic policies and the meaning of human labor. The Presbyterians:

> As our economy continues to evolve, we will have to advocate not just more jobs, but better jobs, jobs that are exciting and fulfilling. Moreover, we will have to rethink the meaning of work.[7]

The Lutherans:

> Work, the expending of effort for productive ends, is a God-given means by which human creatures exercise dominion. Through work, persons together are enabled to perpetuate life and to enhance its quality. By work they are both privileged and obligated to reflect the Creator whose work they are.[8]

In their call for work to be available, humanizing, and expressive of human dignity, these religious leaders are taking significant first steps in recalling their communities to accountability to principles and values central in the Christian message. Theologically, new ground must be forged in developing an understanding of work which is just and compassionate and builds community, rather than destroys it. However, if theological reformulation is to bring change, it must become part of the public discussion; it must find its way from the rarefied atmosphere of theological academia into the common currency.

In this task we must return to familiar symbols. For a change to occur in our public philosophy about work, the new understanding must be articulated in terms that are rooted in our shared experience. The rhetoric of change must be radical in the truest sense of the word—a return to our roots—if it can be expected to take hold. A new work ethic must in fact be an *old* work ethic, a resurrection of the understandings and language which are still familiar, even if now buried under the layered realities of the contemporary economic condition.

It is appropriate to return to the notion of vocation. The term itself has been a recurring theme in reflection on work in Judeo-Christian theology. In the early history of the church, vocation came to be identified with full-time ecclesiastical service. In a dualistic approach to occupation, the few were chosen, through a mystical experience of "calling," to lead and serve in the church. Religious vocation set men and women apart from their peers and led them literally *out of* the mundane struggles of society. The ideal of the monastic life was the attainment of a purely contemplative existence, uncluttered and unchallenged by the "worldly" concerns of the workaday world.

In rediscovering the biblical doctrine of the priesthood of all believers, the Reformation challenged such elitism and otherworldliness. There was to be no special class of individuals who had been called into service: all people were able to participate in the purposes of God through their labor. As John Calvin wrote:

> The Lord bids each one of us in all life's actions to look to his calling. . . . He has appointed duties for every man in his particular way of life. And that no one may thoughtlessly transgress his limits, he has named these various kinds of living "callings." Therefore each individual has his own kind of living assigned to him by the Lord as a sort of sentry post so that he may not heedlessly wander about throughout life. . . . From this will arise also a singular consolation: that no task will be so sordid and base, provided you obey your calling in it, that it will not shine and be reckoned very precious in God's sight.[9]

Despite some variations which developed between the Reformation leaders in their interpretations of vocation, four common assumptions prevailed. These assumptions have survived the upheavals of history and the booms and busts of economies throughout the centuries. They continue to inform the relatively small number of workers in the world who speak of their labor in the context of vocation.

The first assumption is that *each person's work contributes to a greater good,* whether that is primarily understood as bringing glory to God or serving one's neighbor. Human history is evolving, moving in some purposive direction, and every individual can contribute to that purpose. The means of the contribution is one's work.

Second, it is assumed in understanding work as vocation that the work we do is not the means to an end but that the *very activity of work has meaning.* The confirmation of one's vocation should not come at the end of a lifetime of alienated work; meaning is inherent in the daily experience of work, no matter how "sordid and base" the task. Work is not to be random activity—something created to fill our time, keep us out of trouble, or enable us to make our monthly car payments. Rather, each worker should have an awareness of the meaning of her or his labor even while actually on the job.

Third, *vocation is universal;* it is not the privilege of the few. The political import of this democratization of vocation (at least in theory) cannot be minimized. This was at the very heart of the Reformists' agenda—the bold affirmation that all human beings of whatever station in life could participate in implementing the purposes of God. All believers were in fact called into the priesthood, and all their work was considered a form of priestly activity. Unfortunately, this important idea became obscured over time.

A fourth assumption is more problematic—that *vocation is individualistic.* The call of Christ to faith is a general invitation extended to all people, but vocation as it relates to one's work is particularized. What is the task to which *I* am called? For what purpose was *I* created? What would God have *me* to do? For Calvin, one's vocation represented an almost private transaction between creature and Creator—the call to work was solely for the purpose of bringing glory to God. For Luther, faithfulness to one's vocation represented both service to God and neighbor. But for both, and for those who came after them, vocation was a personal decision and act. God distributed individual assignments to individual workers, and only God had a perspective on the sum total.

This interpretation of vocation has endured, at least in religious circles. It has made an impact on Western culture; if truly taken seriously, it could have revolutionized it. For example, the universal right to meaningful work could have been translated into public policy. Instead, it remained within the realm of personal piety and relegated to the category of irrelevance by the majority of the work force, believing or not. It has been the emphasis upon individualism which has taken hold in the culture, fueling, in Max Weber's terms, the "spirit of capitalism" and informing our work ethic.[10]

It is not surprising, therefore, that we have to go to the margins of modern industrial societies such as our own to find a different understanding of vocation and experience of work. Currently in the Philippines, a nation of widespread poverty and tyrannical rule, there is a grass-roots movement responding to pervasive health problems there. In the maldistribution of technology in the world today, the easily controllable diseases of malaria and dysentery continue to be the chief causes of death in that country. The rates of tuberculosis, blindness, and infant mortality are among the highest in the world. The majority of Filipinos (60 percent) now go through life without ever receiving any sort of medical services. As a result, a private move to provide "primary health care" has emerged because of the absence of government concern. In fact it is more accurate to say that it grew out of a traditional culture laden with folk medicine—midwifery, herbal medicine, and a public health care not guilded with professionalism and guarded by a centralized system of credentialing. The new movement of primary health care is really an organized effort to retrieve a health care system that is indigenous to the Philippine culture.

Through a private voluntary effort, Philippine doctors have developed an intensive nine-month training course for local villagers. Participants who complete the training have the approximate knowledge of second-year medical students. In their new role as paramedics, graduates can diagnose basic ailments, vaccinate children, prescribe herbal medication, set broken bones, deliver babies, provide much-needed public education on hygiene, and deliver a number of other basic health services.

According to Dr. Mita Tavera, a major force behind the movement, there is one rule for the participants: *that they share their knowledge with others.* This enables the numbers of new health-care workers to increase and reminds them that their work is not to be an occasion for special status in the village. It also reminds villagers that they are primarily responsible for their own health. The paramedics must be constantly aware that their newfound skills are for the benefit of the community and that it is community needs that determine the work to be done. Their work, in one sense, is not their own. They are dependent on the skills of others who teach them, the trust of their *barangay* (village), and the next generation of health-care workers who are their students. The traditional hierarchical delineation between students and teachers becomes blurred as skills are pooled for the good of the community.

As primary health care spreads, the political ramifications are clear. This is a model of work and education that does not engender dependency or send the message that some are "dumb" and others "smart." Everyone has a calling, a contribution to make, and a role to play. The validation of that calling comes from the community. Skills are shared, collaborative and sometimes interchangeable, therefore empowering the individual rather than creating dependency.

Even as the community brings definition to the individual calling, so this new experience of work brings a deeper understanding of the meaning of community. As health-care workers strive to achieve collective well-being rather than individual self-advancement, they begin to see how their work and their goals are related to the whole social scheme. How can they treat dysentery without addressing the need for improved public sanitation? How can they expect improved social services as long as there is not a democratic political system to hear and respond to their needs?

There is indeed much that we can learn from our brothers and sisters in the third world, those whose work and community life seem so different from our own. Yet it is appropriate that it is they who can teach us from their experience of work and community. There is much that the industrialized countries must learn about work, and some of the answers lie in the "underdeveloped" nations. It is the irony of the new community that those who are considered "foolish" will shame those considered "wise" by the depth of their wisdom.

The new experience of work shared by the primary health-care workers in the Philippines is illustrative of the biblical and theological understandings of human labor. Returning to the roots of that tradition, we find that from its earliest usage *vocation* was never far in meaning from *community*. In fact, the word the early Christians adopted from Greek culture to designate their assembled community was *ekklēsia*, which is built on the root *kaleō*, "to call." At the time, *ekklēsia* did not have any religious or cultic associations but was more of a political term referring to a group of people with a unified purpose and structure. The translation into Latin became *convocatio* —meaning a group "called together."

Thus, members within the Christian community shared a common vocation or calling to serve God and humanity. Within that collective goal, individual skills are matched with particular tasks. But as in the Philippine villages, the future well-being and independence of the community remain primary.

In the apostle Paul's correspondence with one such early Christian community, he exhorts its members to live up to their calling (Eph. 4:1). He then spells out the everyday social ethics that facilitate the smooth interaction of any group of people—cooperation, patience, reconciliation, humility, love, and a constant awareness of common purpose and destiny. Paul goes on to list some of the individual occupations or vocations which are intended to build up the community. Whether one is teaching, preaching, administering, or prophetically working for change, the unity of the community must be served at all times. The common purpose of the community must never get lost in the search for individual salvation or personal achievement. There is a greater cause to be served.

This model of vocation and community has generally been hoarded by the church and even then woefully underemployed. But if the church is to be a microcosm of a global vision for the future, then vocation must be understood in the context of the new community. There must be an awareness that we are not separate and isolated individuals, with a short number of years in which to accumulate as much status and power and money as possible. Rather, we are all part of the public, each of us a member of concentric communities—neighborhood, city, nation, and world. We are an interdependent human community struggling toward a common goal: to make life on this planet decent, just, and indeed possible. Our work represents our contribution to such a future. And that future is not possible without the opportunity and commitment to contribute through vocation to the common good.

Vocation restored to its original meaning and context could radicalize the way we think about our work, experience our jobs, and structure employment in the global society. The call to community comes before career development and corporate profit. Returning to the theological idea of vocation, three of the four assumptions would still hold true. There would be meaning and purpose to human labor. Workers would not sweep streets, teach classes, or make shoes "just to have a job" but in order to contribute to the common good. The universality of vocation would also be recognized. No one would be excluded from participation, and there would be a place for all.

The point of departure from the old assumptions is that, in this understanding, vocation is not individualistic but is drawn from the primary collective call. There is a shared and prior responsibility to the community; individual work is just an expression of that. Personal job choice is not predominantly determined according to "what *I* want and need" but according to what is wanted and needed in the community. The community need must be consciously and publicly defined and not just left to the vagaries of the market, operating in a moral vacuum, or of a lone individual perspective. The myth of *"my"* work then disappears—that distorted perspective that I own my labor, that it is *my* possession, creation, and self-definition.

This possessiveness of labor is not unique to advanced capitalism. As early as the fifth century B.C., the writer of Ecclesiastes tells of a laborer who is driven to despair because she cannot tolerate the thought of the next generation or the second shift tampering with *her* work.

> So I came to hate all my labour and toil here under the sun, since I should have to leave its fruits to my successor. What sort of a man will he be who succeeds me, who inherits what others have acquired? Who knows whether he will be a wise man or a fool? Yet he will be master of all the fruits of my labour and skill here under the sun. This too is emptiness.
> Ecclesiastes 2:18–19, NEB

It is clear that her possessiveness comes not from selfishness, as such, but as a response to alienation, first from her work and then from her community. When people have no control over the "fruits" of their labor, no participation in the decision of a product's distribution and use, no perspective on how their efforts contribute to the community and are appreciated by it, then an abiding alienation takes hold. Workers cannot see themselves as self-in-community, nor their work as work-in-community. Possessiveness is the natural response to this alienation. And this can easily lead to despair. As workers, we want to take pride in what we do; but if we cannot see how the skills of others have aided our work, and how our labor benefits the ongoing community, we become individualistic and speak of "my" work. When we can only see someone else profiting from our labor, we quite naturally want to cling to it and may fall into despair when we discover that we cannot!

When together we own and control our work, when it is seen in the context of the call to community, it becomes the work of us all. Then everyone's work is honored. The community ensures that everyone who wants to work may and that everyone who does work is rewarded justly. Individuals again become the subjects of work and not, as commodities, its objects. In a word, solidarity is restored to our cultural and individual understanding of work.

Vocation as a "call to the common good" is, of course, an ideal. But is it possible for a society as steeped in individualism as ours to have its public philosophy of work transformed? Some of us can recall with fond and insistent memories the years of World War II when the whole country seemed to be working together for a common purpose. From Boy Scout to riveter to entertainer, everyone contributed. Moreover, we have inherited the legacy of an immigrant nation, where, at least in the early generations, private ambitions were deferred while communities were built. Energies were

combined in order to build parochial schools, churches and syna-
gogues, cultural institutions, and shared housing.

The optimist perceives in these examples glimmers of hope that
a change of consciousness about work is possible. A more pessimis-
tic interpretation sees them as limited by their scope and contexts.
Nevertheless, the questions raised by the examples of vocation-in-
community must be asked if they are to instruct us. Whether we see
them as signs of hope or aberrations of the norm, we must ask: Is
a work ethic that emphasizes solidarity among workers and the
common good as its goal *possible* outside of the shared experience
of economic hardship in a developing country, immigration, or a
state of war? These questions must be tested in our culture.

What is more immediately clear is that change *is* needed. Our
philosophy and experience of work has strayed far from its original
context in community. And with the loss of that awareness has come
a deterioration of justice in work. We cannot wait for a change in
public consciousness before seeking change in unjust structures.
(That will both fuel and result from the process.) But for this to
happen we must ask and answer the question: What is justice in
work?

8

Justice in Work

All animals have needs in common for sustenance, warmth, and health. But we must add to these a specifically human need, a need humans have for meaning. It is shared meanings, not shared instincts, which establish community and make it possible for us, as humans, to cooperate in an uniquely complex way. Other living things display in their own fashion great ingenuity and grace in acquiring the necessities of life. But humans, as self-aware and intentional beings, are skilled in a more fundamental and a more fragile way.

This means that justice in work requires not only that the material outcomes of work must be sufficient to sustain life but that the way we do our work—the *structure* of work—must be just. Work that is just should (1) be meaningful—supporting meaningful community, (2) be participatory, and (3) reflect the priority of shared skills. We will examine each of these in turn.

Meaningful Work

Why must work be meaningful in order to be just? When the way we do our work begins to undermine the meanings we share, it begins to contradict the logic of how we humans live. This can happen in either of two ways. The way work is related to the wider society can change so suddenly and radically that moral intelligibility is lost and people "forget" how and why they should be decent to one another. Or the relationship of workers to their work in the narrower work environment can become unintelligible ("meaningless") because of poor design.

This kind of violation of meaningful work is widespread today. We find illustrations in the slums surrounding the rapidly expanding cities of the third world and also in the most sophisticated technical environments of the first world. Both illustrate the same misunderstanding of what human work is all about. Work is not, fundamentally, about making a living or a profit but about how we dwell together meaningfully and well. We tend to ignore this fact, so that work, which seems to be very different in the third world and in the first, becomes unjust in both places for the same reason. Take Nigeria as an example.

"The people live in filth and squalor here. They come from the rural areas thinking their lives will be better, and they end up here."[1] The speaker is Sister Teresee Marques. And the "here" she is speaking of is the Marako slum outside Lagos. Fifty thousand inhabitants live in mud-walled tin-roofed huts there, and an open sewer runs in front of every dwelling. Planks are thrown across the filth so that people will not have to wade through it. But in the rainy season, when the streets flood, there is no escaping.

For all its filth and poverty, Marako has increased its population more than ten times in the twenty years since Sister Teresee first moved in. As she explains, "The people do not think of how difficult their lives are or what is happening to their values. They see the riches of the city and hope for them. They think it's progress."

But what good is progress when its price is the undermining and overwhelming of people's values? "The basic standards of conduct were swept away," says Stanley Macebuh, editor of the *Guardian* newspaper of Lagos. "We developed a culture of individuals. Add to that the sudden explosion of so-called wealth from oil, and everyone just went mad. We have become a far more vulgar nation, coarse in our moral sensitivities, and cynical. Making money has become the sole and only ambition."

Whether in Lagos or São Paulo or Manila or Seoul, a strange story is beginning to unfold, a story that few people anticipated. It is the story of work that is becoming unjust, in the sense of destroying patterns of human meaningfulness, destroying patterns of dwelling together that secure a place for conscience to take hold.

We forgot, or perhaps never fully understood, that work is first of all not a way of making money but a way of cooperating. Meaningful community, in which common decency comes to be expected, is lost when work is too suddenly changed. The individualism and isolation we saw growing in Johnstown, where a traditional industrial city and its culture are staggering toward collapse, is reenacted in third-world cities that thought only benefit would follow from the rapid influx of foreign capital. It is not only Dave Kay in Johnstown who complains of the loss of social cohesiveness but Mutiru Olowu, a third-generation inhabitant of Marako, Nigeria. "Before so many people came, this village was clean. People knew one another and were of one tribe. Now we cannot talk to one another. People do whatever they like." Pointing out the window to an overflowing sewer in front of his house, Olowu remembers better times and sees how, contrary to expectations, economic development has not brought human development.

"That sewer was clogged long ago. I called a meeting of the people and said, 'Let us bring shovels and work together and clean this place.' In the village [that is, Marako before its rapid growth] we would have worked together and done it willingly. For it would have been for the good of us all. But no one here helped. And now all of us suffer together."

When work becomes unjust it is not poverty that is its central or necessary symptom but the collapse of a sense of shared well-being. An isolation and individualism grow up. We do not expect much from others, and we refuse to have others expect much from us. We lose a sense of common good that encourages moral discipline and obligation. Rather than bind us together, work drives us apart. Work "makes sense" to us only as an instrument of individual advancement. We no longer learn from our work that we need and depend upon one another.

This contradicts the fundamental logic of the tools by which we do our work. The tool expresses human intentionality, and all intentionality is co-intentionality. The tool expresses the reciprocity of human skills, building up our sense of individual effectiveness through our effective participation in community. Over time we have used tools to transform our way of dwelling together upon the earth, making our tools more and more complex, and thus our way of dwelling together more and more complex. Modern technology is the extension of this history and development, although many do not acknowledge this and make their plans as if this history and reality do not exist.

Human work becomes collaborative, and thus productive of moral relationships, by being understood together. What was lost in Marako, Nigeria, was a way of making sense together. A sudden and profound change in the structure of work shattered social solidarity, leaving people isolated ("we developed a culture of individuals") and without moral continuities ("standards of conduct were swept away").

But it is not just too rapid a change in the milieu of work that can undermine meaningful community and deny justice. The design of technology can also render us unable to make sense of what we do. The accident in the highly sophisticated nuclear power plant at

Three Mile Island illustrates the same denial of meaningful work as was evident in the Nigerian slum. The human consequences of "mindlessly" transformed work experienced in the third world—the loss of intelligibility—were recapitulated in the most sophisticated of technical environments in the first world. In one case it was the *pace* of technological change that left people floundering and unable to establish meaningful community. In the second, as we shall see, it was the *design* of technology that undermined confidence in human effectiveness and skill.[2]

A nuclear power plant is much like a giant boiler. The reactor core heats up as the radioactive rods within it decay. Water that is continuously pumped through the core absorbs both the heat and the radioactivity and so cannot be used directly to create steam for the turbine. Instead, the radioactive water is contained within a closed system of pipes called "the primary coolant system." A second set of pipes, "the secondary coolant system"—pipes that do not go through the core—pick up the heat. It is "clean" steam from this secondary system that runs the turbine.

On March 28, 1979, the accident at Three Mile Island began with a faulty valve in the secondary coolant system that allowed water to leak into an air line, causing a sudden increase in pressure and automatically closing the valves controlling the flow of water. In effect, this shut down the cooling capacity of the secondary system. The basic elements of the accident were now in place. Without water flowing through the secondary system, the primary coolant system began to overheat.

The designers of the power plant had put in place automatic backup devices, which they believed could control such contingencies. But these were designed less to aid than to make unnecessary the diagnostic skills of the human controllers. The result was that the automatic devices began to hinder the operators' task of thinking their way through the unfolding events.

First, the reactor core automatically shut down as rods covered the fissionable material. Next, auxiliary pumps should have automatically fed water to the blocked secondary system. But the two valves operating these emergency pumps were not working. And one of the lights on the control panel that signals this valve failure was covered by a yellow maintenance tag. The operators failed to gather information that was crucial to understanding and responding accurately to the developing crisis.

As pressure began to build in the primary coolant system because of steam produced by the heat, another automatic backup—as it was designed to do—opened a valve to reduce the water flow and thus reduce the pressure; although the pressure was in fact caused not by too much water in the system but by steam being generated from the overheating core. A second failure then occurred. A light signaling the automatic water reduction to the primary coolant system malfunctioned, indicating that the valve had closed again, when in fact it remained open, continuing to decrease the water flow to the core.

The situation, however, still seemed within the parameters of automatic correction. With the valves stuck open, cool water under high pressure was, again automatically, pumped into the primary coolant system. There followed a crucial human error. Seeing the pressure in the primary system start rapidly to build again, the operators responded in terms of their initial understanding of the problem: They acted to reduce the pressure in the primary system by slowing the backup water flow still more. Only at this point did the operators discover that, contrary to their readings of the control panel indicators, water had not been moving through the secondary coolant system.

However, rather than reevaluate their initial diagnosis on the basis of this new information, the operators began to lose confidence in their ability to understand what was going on. This loss of confidence caused them to freeze upon their first conceptualization of the problem. They continued to bring down the water flow to control the "problem" of pressure in the core, when in fact the problem was precisely the opposite—a deteriorating water level that was slowly uncovering the core and threatening meltdown. Instruments had gone awry. But, even more, human conceptualization and confidence in skilled response had broken down.

For the next hour, water continued to drain from the primary coolant system, causing the core to dangerously overheat. This split some of the water into hydrogen and oxygen and caused a large hydrogen bubble to form. In the first days after the accident some scientists were afraid the bubble might explode, releasing highly radioactive gases into the air. Other scientists were afraid the bubble would block cooling water from the core, with the possible China syndrome of intensely hot and radioactive materials burning through the cement floor of the containment building and escaping into the Susquehanna River and, beyond that, into Chesapeake Bay. In short, the drama of Three Mile Island had begun.

What had gone wrong? It was not operator error so much as a failure of technical design, a failure to design the whole system in such a fashion that it would, in a crisis, aid human operators to apply imaginative diagnostic skills and test alternative explanations. The plant was designed to depend more upon automatic technology than upon the direct application of human knowledge and skill. As the accident developed, the operators found themselves adrift in an environment that was not conducive to innovative and responsive human thinking. Because of this, the operators locked on to an early but mistaken interpretation of the problem and were so confused by the sequence of automated events and signal failures that they lost confidence in their abilities.

Put simply, the operators at Three Mile Island could not bring their work under the control of their active understanding. They became lost in a work environment that was not designed to fit the requirements of human intelligibility—in much the same way as the inhabitants of Marako, Nigeria, found their structure of work suddenly turned against their attempts at understanding and control. "Everyone went mad," complained the newspaper editor. And in a not too different way, people at Three Mile Island also lost their bearings.

Thus definitions of economic development that concentrate solely upon economic outcomes and ignore the collaborative purpose of work can make humans "poor"—disoriented and demoralized—even while improving the level of their material well-being. A theory of economic development can be established accurately only upon the basis of an adequate theory of human work. For the most part, however, this has remained unrecognized. And this has led to injustices in work in both the developed and lesser developed nations—injustices which bear striking similarities in terms of their underlying logic. It is only by being understood together that work becomes part of human intentionality and enters into that solidarity of co-intentionalities which is human community. "Mindless" change—be it too rapid or wrongly designed—betrays the meaning of tools and of technology. This betrayal is found almost everywhere in the world today.

Participatory Work

Besides being meaningful, work that is just must also be participatory. In the first draft of their pastoral letter on the economy, the American Catholic Bishops assert:

> In line with our insistence on the indispensability of human dignity and social solidarity it is clear that *justice demands the establishment of minimum levels of participation by all persons in the life of the human community.* The ultimate injustice is for a person

or group to be actively treated or passively abandoned as a non-member of the moral community which is the human race.[3]

They speak of this indignity as *marginalization*—being pushed to or left at the margins of society, as one who is not needed. Why is this denial of active participation in society such an important deprivation—especially when food, clothing, housing, and medical care are provided by welfare?

As humans, we are uniquely social beings; our life is shared life. In our adulthood, it is principally by way of work that we enter actively into society, whether the work we do be paid or, as housework still remains, unpaid. Through work we experience ourselves as skilled and useful—that is, as needed by others. It is this experience of competence and collaboration that helps us to grow and to develop our adult conscience.

By participating actively in society we build moral meaning and direction into our lives. We transcend futility and fatalism. We discover that the future is not set in concrete but depends in part upon us—upon what we do.[4] Moreover, through work we learn to depend upon others without becoming simply one-sidedly dependent. We learn that we should be dependable because others count on us, even as we depend upon the dependability of others. Work that is good work expands and develops our conscience, encouraging responsibility for self and others. On the other hand, injustice in work —being denied work or having to work under conditions that demean us—injures and inhibits our moral growth. Being treated as unneeded, we become less accountable. We let our grasp upon our lives loosen. Literally, we become *de*moralized.

Why is this sense of skill and competence so important? Because human behavior is uniquely skilled. As infants, we first learned a particular behavior because, usually, we got what we wanted by using that behavior. Take the case of the human cry. Crying, to be sure, involves a set of physiological functions. But the cry becomes a human behavior precisely when it passes beyond an instinctual and more or less automatic process into a purposeful and purposing event. In crying we are actively intending a consequence rather than passively expressing a need. We intend to be comforted. True, sometimes our cry has been ignored; our intention failed. But our crying first had to succeed—effectively secure comfort for us—or we would not have learned to use crying to get our distress relieved. We laugh and cry because we purpose results. Only because we have been able to take delight in our successes do we become more bold concerning our skillfulness, developing and making more complex our intentional behaviors. Therefore, whatever attacks our sense of skill and effectiveness attacks our human essence—our potential for skill development and for moral growth.

An analysis of human behavior as uniquely skilled provides a ground in fundamental anthropology for the ethical claims of participation. Participation is not some abstract or purely ideal criterion; our skillful interaction with others is the very form and way of our being and becoming human. When as adults we are denied active participation in our society—when we have no work or lose our work and find others finding us without skill or usefulness—we begin to lose trust in our own capacity. Like Tony Longo, we think we are dumb. More and more our problem becomes, not that we are not trained but that we begin to suspect we are not trainable. It is not that we lack this or that skill. We begin to think we are "unskillable"—that we lack the underlying capacity within which particular skills can take root and grow to fruition.

Too rapid a change in the structure of work does not simply deprive a given set of skills of any objective way of taking hold—of "incarnating" themselves in the concrete world. Rather, change that is too sudden can take away what we may call "the bias of skilledness"—confidence in our ability to learn. Once that is gone, programs of job retraining have no place to take root. They are like seeds falling upon barren soil, soil that once was fertile. Those who argue for worker retraining programs must recognize that the pace of technological change must also be controlled. If the pace of change is too sudden, the challenge of retraining can be defeated before it has begun.

This is why job security needs to be an integral part of successful retraining programs. Japan, where major corporations guarantee their workers lifetime employment, has learned this lesson. As a consequence, workers in Japan view new technology not as a threat to their jobs but as an aid to the productivity of an organization which has made a lifetime commitment to them. But this is not the case in the United States, where new technology often means to an established work force the eventual loss of their jobs. In one environment, a lifetime of constant skill development makes sense. In the other, it does not. Job security and worker retraining must be seen as two sides of the same coin.

A fuller exposition of the public policy implications of meaningful and participatory work will be developed in the final chapter. However, a description of two mediating principles—from which particular policies more directly derive—is appropriate at this point.

These are the right to work and the importance of economic democracy.

The Right to Work

Work is not a punishment. It is not, fundamentally, what we "have to do" because without it we do not eat or clothe or house ourselves. However true it is that sometimes we go to work only because we believe we must in order to survive, it remains more true that as humans we need to work. Work expresses a direct human need—the need to contribute our skill and effort and to be accounted as useful by our peers, the need to address the future as those who have some control and voice and do not simply have to submit passively to our "fate." No one knows this better than the unemployed. A steelworker in Chicago comments, "There is a hell and I've been there. It's when a man has a family to support . . . and is ready to work and there is no work to do." Or a machinist from Cleveland says:

I'm a skilled machinist out of work for two years. A European corporation bought our plant, didn't retool, wore out the machinery, and used the profits to build a plant overseas where labor is cheaper. Two thousand people were put out on the streets. Hardly anybody got other jobs. My foreman was fifty-seven. He committed suicide. I hear a lot more stories about wives and kids getting beat up. We don't trust anybody anymore—management, union agents, or politicians.[5]

Work is a human right. It is a right established in the very nature of the human. And when that right is violated by economic structures that encourage the abandonment of workers, a fundamental injustice is committed, not by bad owners but by a bad structure of economic decision-making—one that encourages or even demands such abandonment. Work is a right because, as Pope John Paul II has said, "work is a good thing for man . . . not only good in the sense that it is useful or something to enjoy; it is also good as being something worthy, that is to say, something that corresponds to man's dignity, that expresses this dignity and increases it."[6]

When applying this principle of the right to work to our own society, some conclusions seem apparent. First, generating jobs needs to be a central feature of our public policy. Second, purposefully increasing rates of unemployment as a result of policies designed to control inflation is to be morally condemned. When inflation threatens, it needs to be addressed directly, by means of wage and price controls, not indirectly by an increase in interest rates that increases unemployment. The loss of work or the lack of dignified work is so devastating that it must never be seen as "just another lever" in the complex machinery of the economy. We have a right to work; and society must actively respond to that right with policies which ensure full employment—an issue we will return to in a moment.

The Importance of Economic Democracy

The ethical principle of participation also implies a new emphasis upon economic democracy. As a nation, we have long prided ourselves on our Constitutional and First Amendment rights which make it possible for citizens in our nation to participate actively in the *political* process. We have viewed this freedom as reflecting in concrete political structures a dignity that is ours simply because we are human: "We hold these truths to be self-evident," wrote Thomas Jefferson in the Declaration of Independence. However, we have not matched this political democracy with economic structures that encourage active participation of workers and community advocates in *economic* decisions. Instead, such decisions have been seen as part of "management prerogatives." As the Catholic Bishops' letter points out:

> Although the task of ensuring the civil rights of all remains incomplete, we can rejoice in the legacy of political democracy that has been handed on to us from our forebears. We cannot, however, say the same about the intellectual and institutional resources we possess for the protection of the economic rights of all. They remain in need of development.[7]

Conditions of the new global economy, where profits can abandon the workers and the communities which participated in their production, require us to think in new ways about "who owns the economy." Economic structures are as much a part of "the public" as is the political system. True, private investment and decision-making can lead to efficiency. But it is an efficiency which needs to be held strictly accountable to the wider public good. At present, it is not.

Moreover, even as political participation is a moral good for us because it increases our social awareness and urges us into a wider sense of responsibility, so also economic democracy provides important moral training. As workers and community representatives begin to participate actively in economic decisions—which now are reserved to private managers and investors—a new awareness, a new and wider sense of responsibility, will be encouraged. And managers and private investors too will have their moral sensitivities and horizons expanded as they begin, in a more fundamental way, to wrestle with their responsibilities to the work force which produces the profits and to the communities which supply both workers and managers with civility and shared support.

These are issues few of us have thought about before. They are issues which present a fundamental challenge to our collective creativity. But this challenge is invigorating. It makes our own time as exciting and demanding as was the era of our nation's founding. The Catholic Bishops point to this:

> This economic challenge we all face today has many parallels with the political challenge that confronted the founders of our nation. In order to create a new kind of political democracy, they were compelled to develop ways of thinking and political institutions which had never existed before. Their efforts were arduous and imperfectly realized, but they launched an experiment in the protection of civil and political rights that has prospered through the efforts of those who came after them. We believe the time has come for a similar experiment in economic democracy: the creation of an order that guarantees the minimum conditions of human dignity in the economic sphere for every person.[8]

In our final chapter we shall make suggestions for changes in public policy that will encourage economic democracy. However, it is *changed thinking* about the public—not public policy as such—which is the crucial issue. The reality is that the economy belongs to us all. But in the past we have not thought of this as a reality.

The Priority of Shared Skills

Justice in work, besides requiring that work be meaningful and participatory, also requires that work reflect the priority of shared skills. What we have in mind here is influenced by Pope John Paul II's "priority of labor." In his encyclical *On Human Work*, he writes:

> We must first of all recall a principle that has always been taught by the Church: the principle of the priority of labor over capital. This principle directly concerns the process of production: in this process labor is always a primary efficient cause, while capital, the whole collection of means of production,

remains a mere instrument or instrumental cause. This principle is an evident truth that emerges from the whole of man's historical experience.[9]

This claim is laid in the same positive and fundamental doctrine of work that we too have developed. John Paul places work at the center of human development. "Work is a great good for man—a good thing for his humanity, because through work man *not only transforms nature,* adapting it to his own needs, but he also *achieves fulfillment* as a human being and indeed, in a sense, becomes 'more a human being.' "[10] This view of humans as workers, and the principle derived from it of "the priority of labor," leads John Paul to call for a third way, beyond "materialism"—by which he means a certain kind of Marxist orthodoxy—but also beyond "economism"—that kind of capitalism which reduces workers to pawns in the larger game of pursuing profits. The encyclical speaks quite directly and unambiguously about the inadequacy of such an economic theory.

> There is a confusion or even a reversal of the order laid down from the beginning by the words of Genesis: *Man is treated as an instrument of production,* whereas he—he alone, independently of the work he does—ought to be treated as the effective subject of work and its true maker and creator. Precisely this reversal of order, whatever the program or name under which it occurs, should rightly be called "capitalism."[11]

The authors find themselves in fundamental agreement with this line of argument because it insists that justice in work must first of all be *productive* justice, not simply a just distribution of the goods and services produced by the economy, however desirable that also is. The priority of the human worker over the instruments by which he or she does the work is for us, even as for John Paul II, rooted in the simple recognition of what it means to be human. We have chosen to speak of "the priority of shared skills" instead of "labor" because we want to emphasize that all work is *cooperative*—it is work rooted within the historical continuity of the human community. As workers, we are inheritors who do our work drawing upon the legacy of prior human skills, and through our work we continue and develop that legacy.

This principle of the priority of shared skills has very substantial implications for the present institutionalization of work. The first stage of the developing global economy has meant a profound transformation of the power relationships between owner-managers, workers, and local community. Because of the hypermobility of international capital, not only cities and regions but whole domestic populations are made to compete under the discipline of maximizing profits. The terms of this competition range from national and local wage rates, to monetary and taxation policies, to environmental and worker protection laws, and laws regulating the organization of labor. Workers and their unions, together with local, state, and even national political instrumentalities, find themselves at a distinct disadvantage. Power has shifted decisively toward internationalized capital.

There is an objective struggle in the world today, a struggle for power under the conditions created by the new global economy. This struggle cannot be ignored. Nor can the need to take sides be ignored. There is an objective basis, rooted in justice, for the choice of siding with workers and local communities. We need to modify by public legislation the structure of negotiations between labor and capital, and by so doing change the power realities that determine the actions of the various sides.

One such legislative correction is a federal budget that emphasizes job production. A full-employment policy will increase the power of workers by decreasing the pressure of millions of unemployed and underemployed looking for work and, under such necessities, willing to take work even if by their work they undermine the power of fellow workers and go so far as to help break unions. We will discuss such legislation more fully in the final chapter.

Moreover, we need a social costs impact law which would internalize into corporate bottom-line figures some of the human costs (for example, lost wage taxes) of a factory closing or a sudden work-force reduction. These are costs now inflicted solely upon workers and their communities. Such a law would act in much the same way as the present Environmental Protection Law, only it would be the social environment rather than the natural environment that would be protected by being included in management's analysis of cost-effectiveness. Indeed, something like this has already happened. The Sun Oil Company decided several years ago to reduce sharply the number of jobs at its shipyard in Chester, Pennsylvania—from 4,000 to less than 1,500 jobs in just one year. (Eventually the company sold the entire operation.) Sun Company's management negotiated with the city, and the sum of $3 million was paid to cover the projected loss in wage taxes for a five-year period. A major corporation counted as costs to itself some of the costs of the community left behind.

But, some would argue, such legislation would only make doing business in America even more expensive and force businesses to go offshore more rapidly. We would reply that the price of doing business in America—including selling one's products here—should include responsiveness to the priority of shared skills over profit maximization *no matter where one makes one's products.* The powerful incentive of access to the American domestic market could work a significant inducement to iron out a just relationship with workers and communities here in this country, and not simply flee abroad to other countries which display no such concern for justice.

This recasts the present debate concerning protectionism. What is to be protected are the skills of workers and the communities that support them—not protected from all change, nor from all inconveniences, but protected from injury which takes away their capacity for change. Job security must be seen as part and parcel of worker retraining, because it provides a work environment that supports workers' trust in their skills and in their capacity to learn new skills.

Some will ask, Does not the poverty of the third world morally demand economic development? Our answer is, Of course it does. Some will ask, Does not justice in the global economy require that first-world investment and technical know-how be actively involved in the third world? Our answer is, Of course it does. But then we would ask, Should not the pace and the technical design of this change conform to the dimensions of human skill and the capacity to adapt in both third- and first-world living environments? We think it is this last principle which can guide us as a nation in an increasingly interdependent world. It is a principle that protects human skills even as it seeks to enhance them—both here and abroad.

It is clear that the principles of justice in work—that work be meaningful, participatory, and reflect the priority of shared skills—have profound practical implications. The American Catholic Bishops seem to us quite correct when they see our era as needing the same kind of creativity in *economic* thinking that we enjoyed in *political* innovation during the period of our nation's founding.

9

Better Work

Justice in work requires actions which address the fundamental shift in power—away from workers and communities and toward highly mobile international capital—that has resulted from the new global economy. What this means is that there is no long-term solution to the problems of work in the first world that is not integrally related to how work is done in the third world. Few know this better than unemployed steel and manufacturing workers in North America. However, the lessons they have drawn have been negative and defensive. They see third-world workers as competitors who are taking their jobs away. They do not see that it is shifting international capital that *forces* first- and third-world workers to compete with one another, effectively reducing the power of all workers.

There are three dimensions in this shift of power, and each needs to be addressed if justice is to be restored to work. They represent three different levels of community in which we participate: (1) in the global community, trade relations between the first and third worlds, (2) in our national community, the relationship of government to the economy, and (3) in the local community, worker-management relationships at the workplace. Each dimension involves a complex task of analysis and an even more difficult task of practical politics. What follows, therefore, is necessarily more suggestive than definitive, perhaps more of a vision than a strategy.

The Global Community

How can nations and regions of the world, who relate to each other primarily through the exchange of their work (through trade), be more fairly related? There is a long tradition in Western ethics for reflecting upon such matters. It is called "commutative justice." Its central precept is the moral prohibition against harm. And harm is prevented when there is an equivalence of exchange. What makes for such an equivalence? Or, put negatively, what prevents it? From Aristotle we learn that by having only one seller in the market, a fundamental distortion in the exchange relationship, called "monopoly," occurs. Western ethicists and classical economists all agree on this.[1]

They also agree that market inequalities can take many forms. One of these, given attention by the tradition, is ignorance about the true value of things.[2] In our country, for example, the Security and Exchange laws require that sellers of stocks and bonds provide adequate information ("full disclosure") to potential buyers. Without equal *knowledge* about the value of things to be traded, the exchange relationship becomes distorted. Another inequality in market exchange is a disproportion of power that allows one side to impose the terms of trade upon the other. Whether in ancient laws against monopoly or in more recent justifications for organizing labor, a relative equivalence of *power* has been recognized as necessary. Thus, shared knowledge about the value of things to be exchanged and enough equivalence of power so that neither party is forced to buy or to sell against what they know is in their best interest—both of these are what make for justice in exchange.

What do these principles of knowledge and power mean, practically, for trade relations in the global economy? When a young woman who grew up in a rural village that had no electricity makes computer chips in Singapore, she is not likely to know the meaning and, therefore, the true value of her product in the global market. She used to be able to find immediate satisfaction in her work, as she fed the rice she had grown to her family or sold it to a neighbor. But now she lacks an equivalence of knowledge with the multinational corporation with whom she exchanges her labor for pay. Unless that disparity is changed—by worker education and unionization, for example—or unless that worker is protected by a national government which acts in her interest and welfare, a distorted market will result in her exploitation. This is the moral basis for a vigorous program of education in the third world, especially rural education and, given present employment patterns, especially the education of women. Where a traditional culture does not favor the education of women, justice requires that culture to change.

In many countries self-education projects are already under way, not waiting for government sponsorship. Awareness, after all, begets dissatisfaction and the demand for change in the structure of power. That is why many third-world governments have made rural and worker education a low priority, in effect avoiding it.

As education takes hold it becomes clear to industrial and agricultural workers that only labor that is organized, free to bargain vigorously, and involved with worker education can begin to redress the imbalance of knowledge—and also of power—that distorts the exchange relationship between third-world workers and first-world investment capital. But when some of the huge transnational corporations have annual earnings that exceed the total gross national product of many small nations, how can power—and the dynamics of international trade—be made less one-sided and more fair?

In response to this problem, some analysts have advised third-world nations to withdraw entirely from trade with the first world.[3] The price of this withdrawal is to deny to third-world societies much of the investment capital and technical know-how they need for their own development. We believe that international trade can be fair trade, trade without exploitation, but only if third-world governments bargain with greater determination the terms of that exchange. This presupposes, of course, governments which have at heart the interests of the majority and not just the wealthy elite.

Fair trade cannot be separated from the political struggle in many countries today to establish democratic governments. This struggle is carried on against members of the local ruling class—wealthy landowners and industrialists—and their foreign sponsors who prefer a docile and undemanding work force. This political task of democratic reform cannot always be carried on peacefully. There are powerful and well-armed elites who wish to hold on to their wealth. Economic violence precedes and sets the conditions for political violence. Selling arms to such undemocratic governments —arms often bought with U.S. dollars given as "foreign aid"—only increases government brutality and terror and ensures that the common people will conclude that armed revolution is the only effective path to democracy. In many situations that conclusion is correct.

How does it happen that our American government, in a nation that established itself through a war of national independence, so often ends up on the wrong side of the struggle for democracy in the world today? There is in our national consciousness an exaggerated fear of communism which confuses third-world independence movements with Soviet expansionism. The result is a conceptual tyrannization of the world into a bipolar struggle between East and West, a struggle that is actually of marginal concern to the concrete day-by-day interests of most third-world peoples.

In the face of such distortions, it is important to note that average folks here in North America have a vital interest in the *success* of the struggle for democracy in the third world. The imbalance of power

U.S. workers face is similar to the imbalance workers face in the third world. For example, the Firestone Tire Company is viewed by many Filipino workers as their best employment opportunity. Work there is the highest paid in the industrial strip of Manila. They make one dollar an hour. Meanwhile, in Akron and Detroit, unions are blamed for layoffs because of excessive wage demands. And surely American wages must seem excessive to companies that can pay one dollar an hour elsewhere and not have to invest in health, worker safety, or retirement benefits. The response to this should be the realization that power imbalances in world trade favor international capital and place workers on the defensive worldwide. The struggle for power by workers in the third world, when successful, increases the power of workers in the first world by making transnational capital bargain more fairly.

Where democratic governments already exist in the third world, they can increase their bargaining leverage in trade by giving priority to agricultural development for domestic consumption, and not just to urban enterprise zones where products are made for export. Self-sufficiency in food and a thriving rural economy will help ensure the ability to say no to large corporations. And being able to say no is the beginning of being able to say yes to trade that is just. Healthy agricultural development means an independent and viable internal economy, which blocks an export dependency that can be used by international capital to extract unfair trade agreements.[4]

In this regard, third-world governments should be careful concerning loans from first-world funding sources, such as the World Bank and the International Monetary Fund. Pressure to repay loans can distort indigenous development by putting emphasis upon exports in order to secure first-world currencies to repay the loans. Obviously, this advice comes too late for many countries already heavily in debt and under pressure by lending institutions to impose domestic austerity programs that emphasize exports. Ironically, these debtor countries have new leverage with which to bargain because of the havoc their possible default would bring upon first-world economies. Debtor nations should use this leverage to join together with other commodity-exporting countries to press for a new international agency to stabilize commodity prices.[5]

The responsibility for the restoration of fair trade does not reside wholly with third-world governments, however. Public pressure in the first world can also be brought to bear on holding international capital in check, as was successfully demonstrated in the Nestlé campaign. An unusual coalition of the United Nations, women's groups, the religious community, and the consuming public orchestrated an effective boycott of Nestlé products, until the company modified its ways of marketing infant formula in impoverished areas of the third world. Although multinational corporations do operate in a category which transcends national loyalties and control, they still can and must be held accountable by the global human community.

Third-world education programs, unionization, and collective bargaining, and an agriculturally focused policy of economic development, together with activities by first-world people sensitive to the issue of global economic justice—these can all help redress the present imbalances of power in the structure of global trade. The result will be to slow down, but not to stop, the growth in the third world of lopsided export-oriented economic development. This slowdown will benefit *all* workers—protecting their skill development and the moral coherence of their communities. There needs to be less transfer of jobs from the first to the third world and more cultivation of the work and human skills already present in both places.

Moreover, by emphasizing rural development, governments make more pleasing and promising the place where most poor people in the third world presently live. Migration to the cities, which often has the *de*moralizing effects upon families and communities discussed in chapter 8, slows down. It is also clear that in this model of development, land reform takes a high priority. The tendency for smaller farmers to be pushed off their land must be reversed. This reversal will require a farm technology appropriate for small-scale farming. Such policies will fit more accurately into the skill development already present in the third world and encourage the further development of those skills. Capital-intensive large-scale farming reduces rural populations to dependency because they lose control over their work. If a peasant family who once used a variety of skills in self-employment have their land expropriated by a large agribusiness, they suddenly find their future in someone else's hands and their daily activity reduced to one repetitive task. They lose a sense of their inherent life skills and capacities. Often they also lose their food. Today in the Philippines 50 percent of the food grown is exported, while 75 percent of Filipino children under five suffer from malnutrition.

Whether in the first world or the third, real economic development depends upon the conscious cultivation of human skills and should not be guided solely by the logic of highly mobile international capital that does not make shared skills or human community its motivating ethic.

The National Community

These changes in the third world need to be paralleled by changes here at home in the relationship of government and industry. Up to this point, we have trusted "the market" to correct errors or deficiencies and to act in our best interests. If prices plummeted or unemployment soared, we believed the free market would act as a keel and restore balance to the tilting ship. But it hasn't always been so. Products that are unhealthy or counterproductive *do* sell. Profit is still made when unemployment rises. Just wages do not necessarily result from a robust and unregulated market.

If enterprise is to be an expression of freedom for all people, more attention must be given to economic planning at the national level. We must be more intentional and future-oriented in the economic choices we make. It is ironic that in any other social venture we would consider it foolish not to plan ahead and count the costs of various alternatives before us. Yet when it comes to the economy, we resist anything smacking of "regulation." Although there are a variety of proposed approaches to the development of an industrial policy, one thing is clear: economic planning is needed.[6] This planning process must be democratic, encouraging the participation of players from all levels and sectors of the economic drama. Its objective must be the creation and maintenance of a just society, rather than a single focus on economic growth.

A logical priority would be to pursue a stabilization of work-force levels by both local and federal governments. At the federal level this means, above all else, a full-employment budget. There is no lack of things that need to be done in our society, should we decide to put people to work. Our roads and bridges need to be repaired. Sewer lines in older cities and aging and unsafe railroad tracks need to be replaced. Parks and recreation facilities, many of them dating back to the public works programs of the 1930s, need to be restored. Low-cost housing needs to be built. Day-care programs, especially for smaller infants, remain in critically short supply. Much of this work can be done by those with few officially certified skills. (We say "officially certified" because in a community-oriented work ethic all people, simply by being human, are seen to have skill and should always be approached as persons already knowledgeable and talented.) That is why a full-employment federal budget, if combined with expanded apprenticeship and job-training programs in both the private and public sectors, could be for millions the first step out of humiliation and poverty into the discovery of what they already are—skilled and talented people.

This positive possibility leads us immediately to acknowledge the negative reality: poverty is on the increase in our society. By the end of 1983, using the government's official definition of poverty, 35 million Americans were poor, with another 20 to 30 million living below any reasonable standards of decency. After declining from 14.7 percent in 1966 to 11.7 percent in 1979, the poverty rate shot up more rapidly than ever before to 15.2 percent in 1983.[7] Poverty means more than not having enough money. It means being denied participation in society as one whose skills are needed. It means to live without recognition, without earned reward. It means to be stigmatized and shunned.

Moreover, this experience of poverty is not distributed evenly across the various groups in our society. Unemployment among minority adults remains twice as high as for non-minority adults. Among minority youth, unemployment is at least 35 percent and perhaps as high as 50 percent. This tragedy of wasted talents, which prepares young lives for a lifetime of wasted energy and wasted skills, cannot be successfully addressed short of a full employment federal budget. As Eleanor Holmes Norton of Georgetown University noted, "Permanent, generational joblessness is at the core of the meaning of the American ghetto."[8]

What does full employment mean? Certainly not a zero unemployment rate, given the constant flow of new people entering the job market and others, by their own choice, changing their jobs. On the other hand, the American Catholic Bishops have observed with disapproval our society's tolerance—indeed, "the growing public and professional acceptance in recent years"—of unemployment rates of 6 and 7 percent. They instead propose that "an unemployment rate in the range of 3 percent or 4 percent is a reasonable definition of full employment in the United States today."[9]

Such a policy would not simply alleviate the suffering of the unemployed, as serious and important a moral obligation as this is. A full employment policy would also tighten up the job market and increase the bargaining power of workers in negotiating with capital managers and owners. In a labor market where there are fewer people who are desperate for work, workers can use the resulting increased leverage to bargain collectively for job security and begin to stabilize jobs and the communities that depend upon those jobs. Economist Jay Mandle of Temple University sees the broader implications of a full employment policy.

To be able to work, as contrasted to being involuntarily unemployed, is to begin to be empowered. This is the case whether seen from the perspective of an individual or more broadly from the viewpoint of the working class as a whole. At the level of the firm this empowerment may mean a greater ability to extract concessions from management with regard to participation in workplace decision-making or in the determination of the quality of the work environment. At a more macro-level the achieving of full employment will facilitate a rejuvenation of the labor movement, increasing its impact on policy formation. Full employment, in short, would tend to broaden participation in the determination of the important decisions made in society, tending to shift the locus of power away from the minority who are privileged to fill such decision-making roles at present.[10]

A full employment policy increases chances of effective participation in decision-making at the workplace and also in society—significant goals of economic democracy.

An important problem arises at this point. Because it increases the bargaining power of labor, a full employment budget may lead labor to demand inflationary wage settlements—wages that do not reflect increases in productivity. Or firms may take advantage of strong market demand to increase their prices and thereby induce labor to bargain for "their share" of the increased profits. These inflationary pressures must be addressed directly—through wage and price controls—rather than indirectly through manipulating the interest rates, which, predictably, drives up unemployment.

In this second dimension of power relationships—the relationship of government to the economy—the centerpiece of legislative action must be a full employment budget combined with wage and price controls.

But local government and the private sector also have an important role to play in stabilizing the size of the work force at the local and regional levels. They do not have to wait for a national consensus to emerge, or for leadership from Washington. Programs of work-force stabilization make a great deal of economic sense, not only for workers and local governments, who depend upon those jobs for their economic well-being, but also for employers. This is a fact known historically from the experiments at the beginning of the nineteenth century by Robert Owen and rediscovered recently by many innovative employers. A recent report by the Work in America Institute summarizes the benefits *to employers* of work-force stabilization:

Induces employees to support continual change and thereby
   makes for a more competitive company
Encourages employers to invest in training and developing
   people
Helps managers, supervisors, and workers to concentrate on
   the common goal: success of the enterprise
Enhances the employer's image in the community
Enables the employer to move rapidly when a business slump
   ends
Reduces the cost of turnover
Preserves skills and maintains productivity
Avoids the costs of "bumping" and related turmoil
Avoids the costs of income security
Avoids the costs of replacing people who leave in a layoff[11]

Individual employer programs for work-force stabilization are
made many times more effective if they are included within regional
planning among local governments and other employers in the
area. Where this happens, workers are not confined just to one
company for work transfer but have a much wider and more diverse
network of possibilities. Here are some programs which facilitate
work-force flexibility and, therefore, employment stability:

Pension portability and other financial bridging
Private and public sector outplacement services and retraining
Area-wide creation of a computer-based job clearinghouse
   with programs to encourage full utilization by potential employers

Several regional programs for work-force stabilization are already
in operation.[12]

Still, commitment by the federal government to employment security is crucial. Take, for example, the area of federal tax law. At
present many of these laws encourage capital investment and technological change *without considering their effects upon employment*. We
agree with the Work in America Institute in their recent call for tax
law changes. First,

when employers seek favorable tax treatment in a merger,
acquisition, or leveraged buyout, they should be required to
show that they have provided appropriately for the security of
regular employees who, through no fault of their own, have
been downgraded or made surplus as a result of the transaction.

Second,

> when employers claim accelerated depreciation of physical
> assets, they should be required to show that they have pro-
> vided appropriately for the security of regular employees who,
> through no fault of their own, were downgraded or made
> surplus as a result of the introduction of those assets.[13]

The principles of justice in work presented in chapter 8 require
that human resources, the protection and development of the
human actors in production, take priority over the development of
capital, the instruments of production. Major sections of the present
federal tax code directly contradict this principle. They ignore employment security and even encourage capital to abandon workers
in search of tax breaks and profits. Such laws should be changed.

These five proposals—a full-employment federal budget, wage
and price controls to protect against inflation, company programs
of employment security, area-wide work-force stabilization plans,
and changes in the federal tax laws—could make significant im-
provements in how work is done in our society. They are improve-
ments that are just, and they reflect a realistic grasp of what makes
for long-term productivity.

The Local Community

In order for the stage to be set for a just and democratic relationship between workers and employers, equity must also be realized
within the overall work force. Just as it was hard to speak of a
political democracy in which women and blacks were not able to
participate through voting, so too it is impossible to imagine a more
democratic economy if great disparities of economic power exist
among the workers who will participate in that economy. Federal
law has set minimum universal standards for voter registration in
order to encourage maximum participation in the political process.
Today, obstructions to voter participation can be challenged on
solid legal grounds. However, when approaching the economy, we
have allowed vast differences between workers to continue, trusting
the market to somehow bring about justice.

How we, as a society, value work and impart economic power is
through pay. Wages received for labor reflect our values about that
person's work and reinforce our perceptions of it. Currently, as is
well known, women earn only 59 cents for every dollar earned by
a man. Although there has been legislation on the books for over
twenty years protecting the right of "equal pay for equal work," the

discrepancy continues between male and female wages. This is largely owing to the fact that, out of the Labor Department's 427 job categories, 80 percent of women in the work force are crowded into 20 percent of the job categories, primarily at the lower end of the pay scale. Jobs such as teaching, nursing, and office work represent a disproportionate number of women and consistently lower wages.

In the debate over pay equity, the issue is not the reality of income discrepancy but its cause and cure. The question arises, "Are these jobs lower-paying because women do them, or because women choose less lucrative work, or because of the market forces of supply and demand?" It is highly unlikely, first of all, that women in such great numbers would deliberately choose to earn less, especially in light of the increasing economic necessity that is bringing women back to the job market.

Many do argue that it is the free market which has set the wages and, if left alone, the free market will rectify the differences. An editorial in the *Philadelphia Business Journal* analyzes the causes and cures of the low wages of those working in a mailroom.

> If all the workers there, men and women, black and white, feel that they are underpaid, then they could use a proven method of redress of their grievances—they could join a union. If the union, with its collective bargaining clout, could not move the company toward higher salaries, *then it should be clear that the workers are being paid what their work is worth.* In that situation, they could use their final and most effective weapon —they could quit. If enough mailroom workers quit, then the company would have to raise its wage scales to attract workers. The free market would therefore correct the inequity.[14]

Extending this argument: if the mailroom workers did not feel free to quit because of the scarcity of jobs available, then they would stay, their wages would remain low, and that would be further confirmation that they were in fact getting paid what the market determined their work was worth. The supply of willing workers exceeded the demand of jobs available, and, being a buyer's market, the price of work was kept low.

However, the "laws" of supply and demand do not operate as indiscriminately as this line of argument would have us believe. For example, in 1981, full-time registered nurses (predominantly female) were in critically short supply. They earned, at that time, an average of $331 per week. During the same time period, workers in male-dominated fields which did not have a shortage—such as ticket agents, vehicle dispatchers, electricians, and drafters—were earning more than the nurses.[15] How can this be explained by supply and demand? It can't. Obviously, there are other factors operating in the setting of wages.

In a study on job inequity by the National Research Council, commissioned by the Equal Employment Opportunity Commission, it was found that "not only do women do different work than men, but also the work women do is paid less, and *the more an occupation is dominated by women, the less it pays.*"[16] Historically, there has been an inverse relationship between the growth in the number of women in a field, such as that of secretary, and the decline in wages. "Women's work" has simply been valued less in our culture than the labor of men; wages reflect this cultural attitude.

Just as supply and demand has not been the sole factor in creating pay inequity, it cannot be counted on as the remedy. In fact, it seems only to exacerbate the problem. While a shortage of engineers has had a positive impact on wages in *that* field, this has not happened with nurses. Instead, more nurses have been brought in from other countries who are willing to work for less pay when the rising demand would otherwise dictate an increase in earned wages.[17] By artificially increasing the supply, not only women's income but their power to bargain effectively is undermined.

Currently, there is a national effort to compare the "apples and oranges" of different job categories and then to pay equally those jobs of equal value. Critics of the "comparable worth" movement maintain that this is a complex (some would say impossible) task and that pay equity would be costly justice. Both judgments are correct. But however complex and expensive, many state and local governments, as public employers, are pursuing comparable worth as an effective weapon against discrimination. Fifteen states now have laws requiring it for public employees.

The state of Washington, for example, took ten years to do its comprehensive study of pay equity. Looking beyond market forces in calculating the value of a particular job, researchers evaluated jobs according to skill, effort, working conditions, and responsibility. They found, for example, that clerk-typists and beginning warehouse workers ranked comparably in these areas, and yet the warehouse workers, predominantly men, earned salaries 10 pay grades above that of the typists (mostly women). Overall, women working for the state of Washington earned about 20 percent less than did men. In a potential landmark decision, the District Court decided that the state had to pay women what their work was worth. If this decision is ultimately upheld, compliance will cost the state of

Washington $695 million. Even at that price, injustice in work comes more cheaply in financial terms, but it is infinitely more costly of human dignity.

The significance of comparable worth is far-reaching. Obviously, it is not only women who are ghettoized in the job market. Minorities, youth, older people, and those with physical handicaps are disproportionately represented in low-wage job categories. Equal pay for equal job worth will no doubt benefit these groups as well.

But more basically, the debate has brought the *worth* of human labor into public discussion. It has raised the possibility that there are factors which should enter into the calculation of remuneration for work other than the impersonal forces of the market—an idea mocked by critics as "medieval."[18] It is preparation, skill, risk, and responsibility that should be rewarded by society, not the arbitrary gender draw at the lottery wheel of birth. When it is personal resources and not the fate of one's birth that is rewarded, the motivation to work and to participate actively in society is reinforced. When our pay is determined by factors within our control, rather than forces beyond it, we are empowered. Comparable worth will move us toward justice in work, toward a more vital participation in community.

There are other examples of better work. Although a vision of work that is just, democratic, ennobling, and empowering is often elusive, there are glimpses of it—those few stones in the rushing stream which resist the current that dehumanizes work. They should be held up before us for study, inspiration, and celebration.

The community of Mondragon, in the Basque Provinces of northern Spain, is one such stone in the stream. Earlier in this century, it was a factory town, like so many others, with its social and on-the-job hierachies. A young priest, Fr. José Arizmendi de Nesciemento, who was assigned to the Mondragon parish in 1941, changed all that. He began teaching the children of factory workers five years after Franco took power. As the climate became more and more repressive, he spoke to his students of justice and human dignity, of democratic participation and individual freedom—lessons which they internalized.

Five of his students went away to the university and later returned to Mondragon as engineers. Now working for the factory that had employed their parents, they made a proposal to the board of directors that would begin to incorporate the workers into the ownership and management of the company. This proposal was, after all, a logical application of the values they had been taught by their priest. When the board roundly refused such a change, the men, in collaboration with Fr. José, set out to establish a parallel worker-owned factory.

Fr. José had been doing research of his own, reading about English experiments in industrial cooperatives, such as Robert Owen's conversion of a rundown and failing Scottish cotton mill into a successful worker-owned enterprise in the early nineteenth century. Learning from these earlier experiences, Fr. José and his former students organized their first appliance factory around the Rochdale principles—a set of guidelines for worker-owned and -operated companies named after the site, in northwest England, of an early cooperative based on Robert Owen's theories. These guidelines ensure that the structure of the cooperative is not a linear hierarchy but that the management is democratic, with all workers having equal access to power and with pay differentials sharply reduced. Responsibility is ultimately held by the general assembly, a representative body in which each worker has a single vote.[19]

Financed through employees and individual investors in the community, the Ulgor plant operated in the black from its opening in 1958. Its success fostered not only its own expansion but the development of other manufacturing cooperatives. As these began to proliferate, it became apparent that a financial institution supportive of worker cooperatives was needed—so the various factories cooperated in establishing their own bank. Profits made in the community, owned by the community, now began to stay in the community for reinvestment. Next came a cooperative insurance company and a research-and-development component to introduce new products and technologies. A technical school and an engineering university were opened, free to community residents.

In less than thirty years, Mondragon grew to present a sleek skyline of over eighty industrial cooperatives. None of them has failed, and all of them can boast higher productivity and profit than their more traditional counterparts elsewhere. Over 17,000 people are employed by the cooperatives of Mondragon, with no one factory having more than 500 employees/managers/owners, to ensure effective worker participation and social cohesiveness.

Mondragon dramatically demonstrates that there *are* alternatives to a number of the dynamics we have seen operating here in our own country, which make so much of our work bad work. Isolation on the job is broken down as workers genuinely participate in the management of the plant and benefit from its profits, not just by wages but by the community's continued ownership of capital for reinvestment. It is the community, not a privately owned bank or insurance company, that decides where new investment is to be made. Thus workers decide together what work they will do in the future and are able to protect the financial basis of their community.

Competition is eroded by the employment security the cooperatives offer. Worker-management relations are eased by virtue of the fact that the highest-paid worker never makes more than three times what the lowest-paid employee earns. Moreover, the general manager is ultimately accountable to the workers, who are also the owners, with the power to hire and fire. A designated percentage of the profits from the eighty-odd cooperatives of Mondragon is set aside each year for community reinvestment—parks, recreation programs, day-care centers. The whole community becomes the active agent of its present and future well-being rather than the passive recipient of paychecks. It becomes self-determining rather than the object of the decisions of a transnational corporation— decisions that force communities here and abroad to compete against each other for lower wages and taxes, and fewer regulations. When control remains localized, community interest is at the heart of every decision.

This is not to say that there are not problems at Mondragon. Currently, it is addressing the issue of job design to ensure that work is not demeaning, boring, and repetitive. It must also dismantle some of its sexist policies, which up until now have limited the participation of women. And although there is a high level of worker satisfaction, unions—a time-honored protection for dissenters— have not been allowed to organize.

In spite of this, Mondragon is a city transformed. Once permeated with the dreams and disillusionments of a society where owners were not workers and workers were not owners, it is now a community in which cooperation has become a way of life. When a grocery store is needed in a neighborhood, a cooperative is organized. When parents are in need of affordable child care, they think first of cooperatives. Housing is built not for the profit of a few but cooperatively, with the community's quality of life in mind.

Mondragon stands as a symbol that better work is possible. It belies the claims of pessimists that the only human instinct that can be trusted to guide economic policy is self-interest. Collaboration, community, the reciprocity of shared skills, gratitude for gifts given by generations of past workers, a sense of responsibility for our own contribution to the legacy of human work—these are not only ideals ahead of us but also realities behind and around us.

Recognizing this truth makes all the more difficult our sense of the present drift of things—that we are becoming a nation more and more divided into those who have and those who have-a-lot-less in a world dominated by transnational corporations which abandon neighborhoods in their solitary search for competitive advantage. But change begins with the subversive notion that none of this is inevitable, that work can be better work, that the future takes its rise out of the fundamental reality that work is human being and human becoming—our response to the divine invitation to be co-laborers in the ongoing work of creation.

Notes

Preface

1. We are aware that the term "third world" connotes an invidious comparison—falsely, we believe—when put alongside so-called "first world" societies. But the other popularly used designations, such as "lesser developed" or "developing" as compared to "developed" nations also carry invidious connotations. Therefore we have decided to use, throughout this text, the most common form of reference, acknowledging its inadequacy.
2. *On Human Work,* St. Paul Editions (Daughters of St. Paul, 1981).

Chapter 1: Conscience and Economics

1. Personal quotations, unless otherwise noted, are taken from oral history material gathered by the authors or from the transcript of the television documentary entitled "When a Factory Closes" produced by WITF-TV (Harrisburg) in association with the Center for Ethics and Social Policy (Philadelphia) and shown on the Public Broadcast System in November 1983.
2. See George T. Silvestry, John M. Lukasiewicz, and Marcus E. Einstein, "Occupational Employment Projections Through 1995," *Monthly Labor Review,* vol. 106, no. 11 (Nov. 1983), pp. 45–46.
3. From Episcopal Commission for Social Affairs, "Ethical Reflections on the Economic Crisis," *Canadian Ecumenical News,* Feb.–March 1983, p. 1.
4. Max Weber gives a suggestive analysis of this in his book *Ancient Judaism* (Free Press, 1952) and also in his *Sociology of*

Religion (Beacon Press, 1964). Emile Durkheim also explored the change in consciousness that accompanied the rise of city dwelling in his *The Division of Labor in Society* (Free Press, 1947).

5. *Writings of the Young Marx on Philosophy and Society,* tr. by L. D. Easton and K. H. Guddat (Doubleday & Co., 1967), pp. 287–301.

6. Adam Smith, *An Inquiry Into the Nature and Causes of the Wealth of Nations,* 1776, bk. IV, ch. 2.

7. There is another side to Adam Smith's thought about human relationships in society. It becomes evident in his earlier work, *The Theory of Moral Sentiments* (1759), where he makes it clear that society, including market exchange as organized by free capital, remains dependent upon moral virtues that only cooperation, not competition, can supply. However, Smith is best remembered, and therefore most influential, for the kinds of sentiments expressed in our previous quote on the "invisible hand."

8. Quoted from E. F. Schumacher, *Small Is Beautiful* (Harper & Row, 1973), p. 24.

9. See Galbraith's *Economics and the Public Purpose* (Houghton Mifflin Co., 1973).

10. Quoted from Douglas Bauer, "Why Big Business Is Firing the Boss," *New York Times Magazine,* March 8, 1981, p. 88.

11. The most graphic illustration of this is to be found in the novel *One Hundred Years of Solitude* by Gabriel Garcia-Marquez.

12. From the transcript of the television documentary "When a Factory Closes."

Chapter 2: A Culture of Disappointment

1. Michael Lewis, *The Culture of Inequality* (University of Massachusetts Press, 1978).

2. *Culture of Inequality,* p. 43.

3. *Johnstown Magazine,* July 1983, pp. 9, 13.

4. Ibid., p. 9.

5. Ibid.

6. *Philadelphia Inquirer,* October 25, 1984, p. 20-B.

7. Figures cited from the *Detroit Free Press,* "Most Baby Boomer Pockets Aren't Booming," by Jon Margolis, July 1985.

Chapter 3: Blue-collar Blues

1. Quoted from Dorothee Soelle, *Suffering* (Fortress Press, 1975), p. 70.
2. From "When a Factory Closes" (see chapter 1, note 1).
3. From an interview first published under the title "The View from Below" in *Christianity and Crisis,* April 17, 1978, pp. 88–92.
4. The standard work in this area is M. Harvey Brenner's *Mental Illness and the Economy* (Harvard University Press, 1973).
5. Besides Brenner, see Banagale and McIntire, "Child Abuse and Neglect: A Study of Cases," *Nebraska Medical Journal* 60, no. 10 (1975); also B. Nichols, "The Abused Wife Problem," *Social Casework* 57, no. 1 (1976):27–32.
6. Besides Brenner, see A. Pierce, "The Economic Cycle and the Social Suicide Rate," *American Sociological Review* 32 (1967): 457–462.
7. Besides Brenner, see A. F. Henry and J. F. Short, Jr., *Suicide and Homicide* (Free Press, 1954).
8. Besides Brenner, see A. R. Bunn, "Ischemic Heart Disease Mortality and the Business Cycle in Australia," *American Journal of Public Health* (Aug. 1979), pp. 772–781; also, Catalano and Dailey, "Economic Predictors of Depressed Mood and Stressful Life Events in a Metropolitan Community," *Journal of Health and Social Behavior* 18 (Sept. 1977): 292–307.
9. Besides Brenner, see M. Droughton, "Relationship Between Economic Decline and Mental Hospital Admissions Continues to Be Significant," *Psychological Reports* 36 (1975): 882.
10. As quoted by Barry Bluestone, "Deindustrialization," in *Community and Capital in Conflict,* ed. by John C. Raines et al. (Temple University Press, 1982), p. 46.
11. Bureau of Labor Statistics Report, July 1984. Quoted from the *Philadelphia Inquirer,* August 19, 1984, p. 8-D, "Despite the Recovery, the Recession Lingers for Many."
12. Quoted from an unpublished paper by Barry Bluestone entitled "Whither the Middle Class? Labor Market Prospects for the Decade Ahead," p. 5.
13. See Richard A. Easterlin, *Birth and Fortune: The Impact of Numbers on Personal Welfare* (Basic Books, 1980).
14. See Linda Snyder Hayes, "Youngstown Bounces Back," *Fortune,* December 17, 1979, as quoted by Bluestone (see note 10), p. 46.

15. See "Recovery Bypasses Millions," *Just Economy,* vol. 2, no. 3 (July/Aug. 1984), pp. 1–2.
16. Quoted from "When a Factory Closes."
17. See "Capital Flight and Job Loss" by Arthur Hockner and Daniel M. Zibman in *Community and Capital in Conflict: Plant Closings and Job Loss,* ed. by John C. Raines et al. (Temple University Press, 1982).
18. From "Hard Times and Tight Budgets in Chester City," by Robin Clark, *Philadelphia Inquirer,* November 29, 1984, p. 14-B.
19. Ibid.
20. See Lee Soltow, ed., *Six Papers on the Size Distribution of Wealth and Income* (National Bureau of Economic Research, 1969).

Chapter 4: Her Dream Undone

1. See Kay A. Snyder and Thomas C. Nowak, "Sex Differences in the Impact of a Plant Shutdown: The Case of Robert Shaw Controls," American Sociological Association, August 1983.
2. Ibid. See also Barry Bluestone and Bennett Harrison, *The Deindustrialization of America* (Basic Books, 1982), pp. 54–55, 81.

Chapter 5: The Realities of Social Class

1. This idea of the view from below is similar to the idea of "the epistemological option for the poor" developed by Gustavo Gutiérrez in his *A Theology of Liberation* (Orbis Books, 1972). For Gutiérrez, too, the perspective of the poor upon society is uniquely clear, if they are able to disengage themselves from the established ideology. For an analysis of how oppression leads to the introjection of anger and violence directed at fellow victims, see the classic *The Wretched of the Earth* (Grove Press, 1965) by Frantz Fanon.
2. That the working class seeks to defend its self-esteem from the value system of competitive individualism is examined by Jonathan Cobb and Richard Sennett in *The Hidden Injuries of Class* (Alfred A. Knopf, 1972). We view this attempt as more successful than do they.
3. The classic study of how the working class repeats itself not only biologically but sociologically, reproducing in the next generation its relationship to other classes, is Edward P. Thompson's *The Making of the English Working Class* (Pantheon, 1964).

4. The importance of naming one's own reality is developed brilliantly by Paulo Freire in his *The Pedagogy of the Oppressed* (Seabury Press, 1971). Dorothee Soelle develops the same idea in terms of lamenting and "crying out"—as in prayer—in her book *Suffering* (see chapter 3, note 1). The self-liberation from silence and muteness and the epistemological task of "naming one's situation" is used by the church in the base communities in Latin and South America.

5. This interview was first published in the journal *The Other Side*, November 1979, under the title of "Charlotte's Story."

6. This interpretation of the commandment to "love thy neighbor as thyself" is developed by Gutiérrez (op. cit., note 1), where he shows that it is precisely the oppressed who possess the perspective upon social reality the rest of us need in order to gain moral clarity.

Chapter 6: Work and Democracy

1. John Locke, *Second Treatise of Government,* ed. C. B. Macpherson (Hackett Publishing Co., 1980), p. 29.

2. Ibid., p. 24.

3. Ibid., p. 8.

4. Quoted from *The Complete Essays and Other Writings of Ralph Waldo Emerson,* ed. by Brooks Atkinson (Modern Library, 1940), p. 163, emphasis added.

5. Ibid., p. 169.

6. Quoted from an essay by John Updike entitled "Emersonianism," *The New Yorker,* June 4, 1984, pp. 113 and 116.

7. Ibid., p. 117.

8. Emerson, *Complete Essays,* p. 160.

9. Ibid., p. 149.

10. In her book *In a Different Voice* (Harvard University Press, 1982), Carol Gilligan says of this gender bias (p. 156), "Male and female voices typically speak of the importance of differing truths, the former of the role of separation as it defines and empowers *the self,* the latter of the ongoing process of attachment that creates and sustains the *human community.*"

    It is clear from what we have said that in our view our culture needs to hear from and listen to women and what women have learned from the work they have done in the conventional division of labor: the nurturing of attachments.

11. Quoted from *The American Puritans,* ed. by P. G. E. Miller (Doubleday & Co., 1956), pp. 83–84.

12. Quoted from Stephen B. Oates, *Let the Trumpet Sound: The Life of Martin Luther King, Jr.* (Harper & Row, 1982), pp. 256–263.

13. Quoted from a book review in the *Philadelphia Inquirer* by Catherine Barnes entitled "A History of Racism in Dixie" (Book Review Section, Sunday, December 2, 1984, p. 7).

Chapter 7: Vocation and Community

1. See Max Weber, *The Protestant Ethic and the Spirit of Capitalism* (Charles Scribner's Sons, 1958).

2. Quoted from Liston Pope, *Millhands and Preachers: A Study of Gastonia* (Yale University Press, 1942), p. 22.

3. See Weber, *Protestant Ethic*, pp. 128–139.

4. See James H. Cone, *The Spirituals and the Blues* (Seabury Press, 1972), p. 122.

5. Ibid., pp. 123–128.

6. "Catholic Social Teaching on the U.S. Economy, First Draft of the U.S. Bishops' Pastoral Letter," para. 158, *Origins*, 40, no. 22/23 (Nov. 15, 1984), p. 358.

7. Quoted from "Toward a Just, Caring, and Dynamic Political Economy," Presbyterian Church (U.S.A.); adopted 1985.

8. Quoted from "Economic Justice," a social statement by the Lutheran Church in America; adopted 1980.

9. John Calvin, *Institutes of the Christian Religion* 3.10.6, Library of Christian Classics (Westminster Press, 1960).

10. See Weber, *Protestant Ethic*, chapter 2.

Chapter 8: Justice in Work

1. This and the following quotes are taken from an article written by Robert J. Rosenthal entitled "How Nigeria Missed Its Big Chance," *Philadelphia Inquirer Magazine*, December 30, 1984, pp. 17–19.

2. The description of the accident at Three Mile Island and the understanding of that accident as resulting from a failure of design is indebted to Larry Hirschhorn's *Beyond Mechanization: Work and Technology in a Postindustrial Age* (MIT Press, 1984), ch. 8.

3. "U.S. Bishops' Pastoral Letter," para. 92 (see ch. 7, note 6; emphasis added).

4. This "de-fatalization" of the future is one of the key concepts developed by Freire and Gutiérrez. It is liberation from being

a passive object of history, part of history somebody else is writing, to becoming an active subject.

5. Quoted from The Great Lakes/Appalachian Project on the Economic Crisis, *Building Justice in Communities* (Cleveland, Ohio, Dec. 1984), pp. 1–2.

6. *On Human Work*, p. 23 (see Preface, note 1). It is important to note that the theory of justice we are using here, and the language of workers' having a right to work, derives from our sense that human beings are fundamentally social. The right to work has to do not with autonomy but with relationship; it is not a right to be protected from the interference of others (the state, for example) but a right to full membership in the group. It is close to what Jurgen Habermas means by "communicative justice," competence in social intercourse (see his *Theory of Communicative Action*, vol. 1 [Beacon Press, 1984]).

7. "U.S. Bishops' Pastoral Letter," para. 84 (see ch. 7, note 6).

8. Ibid., para. 89.

9. *On Human Work*, p. 25.

10. Ibid., p. 23.

11. Ibid., p. 18.

Chapter 9: Better Work

1. See Aristotle, *Politics* 1.11.1259a.

2. In thinking through the issue of justice and exchange, we have found very helpful an unpublished paper by Professor Jon Gunnemann of the Candler School of Theology at Emory University, entitled "Capitalism and Commutative Justice."

3. For a statement of this point of view see Thomas Weisskopf, "Capitalism, Underdevelopment and the Future of the Poor Countries," in J. N. Bhagwati, ed., *Economics and the World Order: From the 1970s to the 1990s* (Macmillan, 1972).

4. See Joseph Collins and Frances Moore Lappe, "Food Self-Reliance," in John Galting, Peter O'Brian, and Roy Preiswerk, *Self-Reliance: A Strategy for Development* (London: Bogle-L'Ouverture Publication, 1980), pp. 140ff.

5. See the "Introduction" by J. N. Bhagwati in Bhagwati, ed., *The New International Economic Order: The North-South Debate* (MIT Press, 1977).

6. Unpublished presentation by Norman Faramelli to IECON (Interreligious Economic Crisis Organizing Network), Sep-

tember 1983, and Boston Theological Institute Ethics Group, February 1984.

7. U.S. Bureau of the Census, Current Population Reports, Series P-60, No. 145, U.S. Government Printing Office, 1984, p. 20.

8. From Holmes, "Restoring Black Families," in the *New York Times Magazine,* June 9, 1985.

9. "U.S. Bishops' Pastoral Letter," para. 179 (see ch. 7, note 6).

10. From "The Achieving of Full Employment," p. 9, forthcoming in *Socialist Review.*

11. Quoted from *Employment Security in a Free Economy,* A Work in America Institute Policy Study, directed by Jerome Rosow and Robert Zager (Pergamon Press, 1984), p. 4.

12. The "Twin Cities Human Resource Planning Council" is one instructive example.

13. Ibid., pp. 11–12, emphasis added.

14. *Philadelphia Business Journal,* September 3–9, 1984.

15. "Pay Equity on Trial," American Federation of State, County, and Municipal Employees (AFSCME), 1983, p. 9.

16. As quoted by the *New York Times,* September 4, 1984, p. B9, "Equal Pay for 'Comparable Worth' Growing as a Job-Discrimination Issue," by Walter Goodman, from a report by the National Research Council commissioned by the Equal Employment Opportunity Commission in 1981.

17. Ibid.

18. Ibid.

19. *Mondragon,* TV documentary produced by BBC in 1981.

Index